The Soft Toy Workbook

The Soft Toy Workbook

Judith Duffey and Phyllis Ford

B. T. Batsford Ltd, London

ISBN 0 7134 6123 3 (cased)

Typeset by Deltatype Ltd, Ellesmere Port, Cheshire
and printed in Hong Kong

for the publishers
B. T. Batsford Ltd
4 Fitzhardinge Street
London W1H 0AH

Photographs by Sue Atkinson

Contents

1 Introduction

The patterns in this collection represent what we believe to be a new and unusual approach to soft toy making. The designs came about as a result of mutual interests as diverse as quilting, sculpture, natural history and teaching. We were looking for ways of creating entertaining small projects for quilters as well as trying to develop ways of making solid fabric forms without stuffing. We were fascinated by the way the regular geometric forms and textures of quilting appeared in natural forms; at the same time we were interested in developing teaching toys that could be used in a variety of ways to encourage imaginative play and specific manipulative and perceptual early learning skills. Also, we just liked toys.

It is probably no accident that, of all the toy designs in this collection, the chameleon is one of our favourites. In a way he combines all these features in his various and changable personality. His coat changes colour in the order of the spectrum like the leaves of a book; his ruff is a quilting pattern straight out of nature's notebook; the structures of his feet and tail demonstrate new ways of manipulating fabric forms. His adaptability as a teaching toy as well as his appealing shape and personality sum up our approach to soft toy design.

In a way, many of the toys you'll find here are chameleon-like. Each has some new or unusual characteristic, either in technique or in the possibilities it offers for flexible play. While some patterns incorporate the familiar traditional soft toy construction of filling a seamed three-dimensional fabric form to give it shape and solidity, most are based on another principle: the assembly and manipulation of separate flat, padded and quilted shapes.

This technique has several advantages: there is no need for stuffing, which can sometimes be a little tedious and messy. Unlike stuffed soft toys, the padded shapes are collapsible and therefore easily portable and washable. Because they take up small amounts of space, they are ideal for travelling. The absence of solid filling means that they are not only lightweight, but dry easily.

Perhaps their most interesting feature, however, is their flexibility. Because they are basically hollow shapes, they can be used in many more ways – as containers, covers or, as in two of our patterns, as stacking toys. The quilted surface also gives them sufficient body and stability to stand alone. While this idea grew partly out of experiments using padded shapes to construct sculptural forms out of fabric without filling them, we have to admit that our primary inspiration was a piece of pitta bread. In this case, playing with our food was particularly productive. We discovered that this hollow half oval could fold flat, stand by itself when opened out, or serve as a container for smaller versions of itself (or anything else!). This idea, which we sometimes refer to as the 'pitta principle', led to new ways of thinking about designing soft toys and new ways of making and using them.

The basic principle of construction is very simple and consists of three main steps. First, flat padded shapes are made by seaming a layer of wadding to two layers of fabric placed right sides together, and leaving an opening for turning. (This is unlike the usual 'quilt sandwich' that places a layer of wadding between two layers of fabric right sides out.) The stitched fabric is then trimmed, the corners clipped, and the piece turned inside out. Corners and seams are eased out from inside; the turning opening is sewn closed by hand. (We find it easiest when working with small pieces to mark and stitch the seam lines on the fabric *before* cutting out; this eliminates one process and allows greater precision in stitching and cutting. For many pieces, it is possible to eliminate the marking process altogether by simply cutting a template to the size of the piece, pinning it directly to the fabric and stitching around it.)

Next, the individually finished padded pieces are quilted as desired, by hand or machine. (It is usually best, especially with large pieces, to tack the layers together before quilting to avoid puckering.)

Finally, the flat quilted pieces are assembled by sewing the edges together by hand or machine, or manipulated by folding, coiling or wrapping. The shape and number of pieces joined will determine the final shape.

The idea of using the stability of quilted fabric to form three-dimensional shapes fits neatly with the idea of using the pieced designs of traditional quilts as parts of the toys. Often the particular pattern was dictated by the resemblance of a quilting pattern to a natural form, as in the hexagons of the armadillo or the turtle shell. The particular pleasure of working on this small scale, with animals or three-dimensional objects, is that only a relatively small number of hexagons is required (making a bed quilt from hexagons is a daunting prospect!) and the results, we find, are more fun and satisfying than oven gloves or place mats. An additional benefit of working with the geometry of pieced and quilted shapes is their value as teaching devices.

We hope that you will use our patterns simply as suggestions and starting points for your own adaptations of favourite quilting and patchwork ideas.

Getting started

Enlarging patterns

Although many of these patterns can be made the size of the pattern piece given, you will probably wish to enlarge some of them, especially the more complex ones.

The simplest and most convenient way to enlarge a pattern is to reproduce it on a photocopier that has an enlarging and reducing facility. Many instant print or photocopy shops offer this inexpensive service.

You can also enlarge the pattern to the desired size by using the grid system. First estimate roughly how much larger you wish to make the toy (i.e. twice, three times) and draw a regular grid whose squares are double or three times (or whatever proportion you choose) the measurement of the squares on the pattern grid. Then, square by square, redraw the pattern on the larger grid by copying the exact placement of the line within the square. (It is often useful to ask yourself questions like 'does the line intersect the edge of the square half-way or a third across or somewhere in between?') You can also use clock angles to estimate locations. For example, does a line curve gently from 8 o'clock to 3 o'clock through the centre of the square? It is, of course, important to be very accurate when enlarging on the grid.

Before starting

First read carefully all the instructions for the pattern you have chosen. Because we are introducing a number of techniques that may be new to you, it is important to read and visualise each process with the help of the explanatory diagrams. We have included illustrations for all complex procedures to make sure the instructions are clear.

You may, of course, discover alternative ways of constructing or assembling shapes: by all means use them. Our aim is not to lay down a series of rigid rules, but to introduce new ways of working with quilted fabric forms.

Note that the pattern pieces *do not* include a seam allowance. The edge of the pattern is the stitching line. This is because we often prefer to use the pattern pieces as templates to stitch around. If you prefer to work with traditional seam allowances, add a regular narrow allowance of about 6 mm (¼ inch) to all sides of the pattern.

Calculating fabric requirements

Because you will probably wish to make the toys in the sizes that *you* choose, and because you may wish to vary the patchwork combinations to suit yourself and your scrap bag, we have not given specific fabric requirements. To calculate the amount of fabric needed for a particular pattern, enlarge the pattern to the desired size. Cut out the pieces. Read the pattern instructions and look at the diagrams to see how many of each piece you will need, and note whether the piece is placed on the straight or the cross grain of the fabric. Lay the pattern pieces out as you would for cutting each colour or print. Measure the space occupied; this is your fabric requirement.

While these toys can be made almost any size you like, you will find that most can be made from small remnants or scraps. Our largest model is about 30 cm (12 inches) long; the smallest about 10 cm (4 inches). No individual fabric requirement was more than half a metre (¾ yard).

Fabric choice

As in traditional quilting, lightweight cottons which hold their shape, keep creases and feel pleasant to touch are the most satisfactory, but any tightly woven fabric that does not fray easily will work. Because there are many small pieces with narrow seam allowances, it is important that the fabric resists fraying. There may, of course, be times when it is worth the trouble to work with other kinds of fabric, like velvet or corduroy, for particular textural effects. But keep in mind that the more loosely woven the fabric, the more likely it is to fray and to create problems. These loose fabrics can sometimes be handled more easily by backing them with lightest weight iron-on interfacing. Experiment with a small piece first.

If you expect to wash the toy frequently, it is a good idea to wash the fabric first to test for colour-fastness and shrinkage. And, of course, it is also important that whatever wadding or filling is used be washable.

Colour choice

Choosing colour is very personal. Above all, choose colours you like. If you are already a quilter, you will already be used to looking at colours in terms of their darkness and lightness ('value') as well as their colour. In general, almost any combination of colours that are identical or similar in value will harmonise. Then, as in quilts, contrasts can be made between the dark and light areas to form patterns. Experiment by trying lots of small pieces in various combinations.

While personal taste is always primary, it is useful to remember that colours can look very different depending on the neighbouring colour. For example, bright red will appear more intense next to a bright green (its complementary or opposite on the colour wheel) than it looks placed against another red. Muted colours will look more colourful against other muted colours. Placing an intense blue next to a more neutralised blue will make the latter appear more grey; but the same muted blue against an orange will appear more blue. Neutral colours are especially 'shifty'; more intense colours vary less in response to their surroundings. Experiment with as many colour combinations as you can.

For small children, you may wish to use primary colours as a way of teaching the colour names.

When working with print fabric, quilters usually like to use small-scale prints so that quilting lines are not obscured. Again, experiment to find the combinations which feel right. Use the reverse side of a fabric if it blends better with your other fabrics.

Pre-piecing fabric

Experienced quilters will be familiar with the techniques of piecing strips before cutting, as in Seminole patchwork. We have adapted a simple version of this in some of the patterns in order to avoid joining many small separate pieces of contrasting fabric. In this technique, two pieces of contrasting fabric are seamed together and the seam allowance pressed open. The sewing lines of the pattern pieces are marked (or the template pinned) on the fabric so that the colour change in the piece (for example between a hand and a sleeve) falls directly on the seam between the two contrasting fabrics.

Pressing

Quilters usually recommend that seam allowances be pressed to one side for additional strength. We have suggested here that most seams be pressed open, since this usually makes handling easier. Use whichever method you prefer, however.

It is very important *not* to press fabric after wadding has been attached, since this will compress the wadding and make the quilting less visible. Press fabric before cutting and after piecing, *before* attaching the wadding.

Machining with contrasting colours

If you wish to make the top stitches stand out more than the bottom stitches, use a colour which matches the fabric in the bobbin and a contrasting thread in the needle. This gives machine stitching something of the character of hand quilting.

Contrasting needle and bobbin threads may also be used where the two sides of the piece to be quilted are of two different colours and you wish to have thread matching the fabric on both sides.

Building three-dimensional shapes

Assembling flat padded shapes

The simplest way to turn flat padded shapes into a three-dimensional form is to seam two identical shapes together part of the way around to form an independent pocket. This can be opened out to form a stable shape, open on one side, which can be made to stand by itself, or serve as a cover or container. (The tea cosy and oven glove are simple functional examples of this principle.)

By combining more than two identical shapes, many different kinds of three-dimensional shapes can be achieved. For example, six equilateral triangles seamed together on two sides each (points meeting at the centre) will form a flat hexagon. Two seamed together will form a pocket; three, a three-sided pyramid shape; four, a four-sided pyramid with a square opening at the base; five, a slightly raised pentagon.

Completely enclosed shapes can be formed by seaming the identical pieces together on all sides, as, for example, in the six squares which form a cube. Combining different rather than identical shapes on all sides allows for endless modifications of the shape. A soccer ball, for instance, is a combination of pentagons and hexagons.

In this way, the basic geometric shapes that are the familiar building blocks of flat quilting can become the units for building all kinds of three-dimensional shapes.

Using the grain to refine the shapes

The stretchy quality of the cross grain in fabric can be used to help refine the shapes, especially in shapes that are unpadded and filled in the traditional way. If, for example, a six-sided filled cube is made from fabric cut on the straight grain of the fabric, it will retain a more 'blocky' appearance than a cube made from fabric cut on the cross. Cross-cut cubes will bulge and soften in response to the pressure from the interior filling and produce a much rounder form. By combining pieces cut on the straight grain and pieces cut on the cross, a considerable degree of control can be exerted over the final form.

Manipulating machined fabric

The shapes of slightly filled or quilted fabric can be altered by manipulating the fabric slightly as it is fed through the sewing machine.

Curves can be built in while topstitching by lifting the fabric into a vertical position as it is fed into the machine. This stretches the fabric more on one surface than the other, and locks in the curve by stitching it in place (see chameleon feet).

In a similar way, wavy or ruffled edges can be achieved by stretching the quilted fabric slightly as edges of the fabric are zigzagged to provide a finished edge. The greater the degree of stretch, the more exaggerated will be the ruffled effect (see Stacking Bunnies).

Solid shapes

While fairly solid shapes like rods or sticks can be produced by packing filling very tightly into a sewn form, a quicker and more effective way is to zigzag heavily over the whole surface of a padded rectangular piece of fabric. The quilted piece, made more rigid by the repeated stitching, can then be folded in half lengthwise and zigzagged again. The process can be repeated until the piece will no longer fit under the presser foot. The final edges can be sewn by hand or by zigzagging along the edges (see Car axles).

Multiplied shapes

The effect of a three-dimensional solid can be achieved by using a series of repeated identical quilted forms which project away from a flat base. This creates an implied solid form in much the same way as a row of dominoes suggests a solid wall.

Coiling

Long padded strips of fabric can be coiled tightly into cylindrical shapes. This works more effectively if the fabric is cut on the cross, as the stretch of the fabric will produce a tighter form (see Car wheels).

Eyes

The easiest way to make eyes is of course, to sew on buttons or beads. For safety reasons, however, these should not be used on toys intended for young children. While alternative eyes can be embroidered in many shapes and sizes, we have developed two special treatments which are both safe and attractive.

Eye no. 1 (Rhino)

Cut a circle of fabric twice the diameter of a penny. Shape it by gathering fabric around the penny with small running stitches. Press. Remove the penny. Press again. Fill with a little wadding. Tack and sew the eyes in place.

Eye no. 2 (Armadillo)

Mark a circle of the size of eye desired on the wrong side of the fabric, or pin a template to the wrong side of the fabric. Place this on a facing, right sides together. Join the circle to the facing, stitching three quarters of the way round. Fill with wadding. Complete stitching the circle. Trim the edges to a narrow seam allowance. On the pattern piece, draw a circle the size of the eye on the wrong side of the fabric. Draw lines across the circle, dividing it into eight equal segments. Clip lines from the centre to the edge of the circle. Fold back the circle segments on the wrong side of the fabric and press. Lay the eye on a flat surface. Place the hole of the pattern piece over the eye. Topstitch around the eye on the right side of the fabric.

Placement of eyes

Experiment with the position of eyes to see how varying the placement changes the personality of the toy. Close together or crooked eyes give a very different (and often quite charming) effect from eyes placed symmetrically and wide apart. The distance from the forehead and mouth also changes the expression radically. Play with placement until you find a personality you like.

About the patterns

We have arranged the toys in three groups according to their construction. The first group consists of patterns combining traditional soft toy-making techniques with elements of patchwork and quilting. The second group contains patterns consisting primarily of assembled flat quilted shapes. Some of these incorporate piecing, but none is stuffed in the traditional way.

In the third group are more complex applications of the padded shape. Here, separate padded shapes are manipulated in various ways before assembling.

In each section, the patterns have been graded according to ease and speed of construction. One star indicates a very quick and easy pattern, which any beginner should be able to handle. A two star pattern will generally require more pieces and more complex structures, while three star patterns should provide a challenge for the more experienced quilter/toymaker.

Glossary of UK/US terms

UK	US
Bias	On the cross
Wadding	Batting
Tack	Baste

2
Rhino **

The tough-hided rhino gets a softer treatment in a separate quilted coat that covers a traditionally stuffed body.

Body

Mark stitching lines of body side, body front, underbody and top of horns on wrong side of print fabric. (Mark body twice, reversing.) Cut out all pieces, leaving a narrow seam allowance. Stay stitch (stitch in seam allowance close to stitching line) all sides of body front and top of horns, and from point **A** to point **B** on body side, to prevent stretching.

Shape eyes by gathering circle of fabric around a penny with small running stitches. Remove the penny, press, and put a little stuffing in the eye. Sew eyes in place on each body side.

Mark ears on wrong side of print fabric. Place on plain fabric, right sides together. Stitch, leaving lower edge open for turning. Trim. Clip corners and curves. Turn right side out. Push out point of ear. Press. Fold and tack ears to body sides as indicated on pattern.

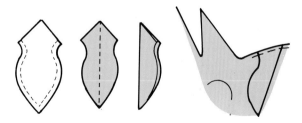

The top of body pattern is divided into two pieces. Tape the two pieces together before marking fabric. Mark shape on wrong side of print fabric. Trim, leaving a narrow seam allowance. With right sides together, stitch body top to one body side, beginning at rear horn. Repeat on opposite side.

Stitch top of horns to horn portions of body sides, matching points **ACCD** of gusset to points **ACCD** on sides.

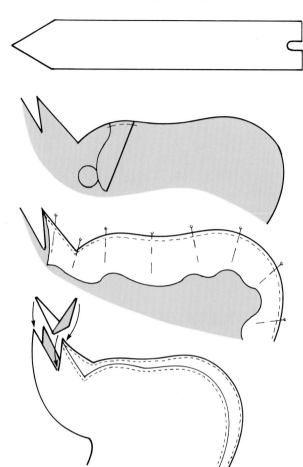

Stitch body front to sides of body, beginning at bottom of front feet. Join points **G** to **D** of body sides, forming front of first horn.

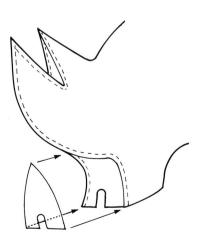

Stitch underbody to sides, front legs and hind legs, leaving opening for stuffing.

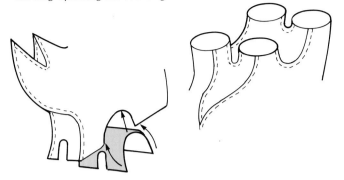

Cut soles of feet from plain fabric, leaving a narrow seam allowance. Tack soles to lower edge of legs. Trim close to stitching. Clip. Turn rhino right side out. Stuff. Handsew opening.

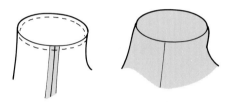

Cut tail from print fabric, leaving a narrow seam allowance. Hem both ends with a narrow hem. Fold lengthwise, right sides together. Stitch along long side, forming a tube. Turn right side out. To finish tail, fold about 2 metres of yarn in pieces twice as long as the tail and draw through the tube. Sew across base of tail to hold yarn in place. Sew tail to body at point indicated on pattern.

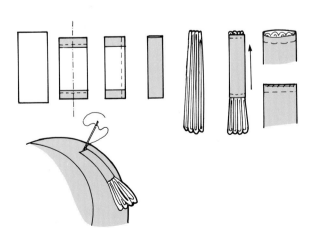

Coat

Mark coat shape on wrong side of plain fabric. Place fabric on matching facing, right sides together. Place both layers on a layer of wadding. Stitch seam, leaving opening for turning. Trim. Clip corners and curves. Turn right side out, easing out points and edges from inside. Handsew opening.

Mark quilting lines on one side of fabric. Topstitch on quilting lines, using contrasting thread.

Slip coat over body. Form rear curves by slipstitching edges of open darts together. Sew coat to body.

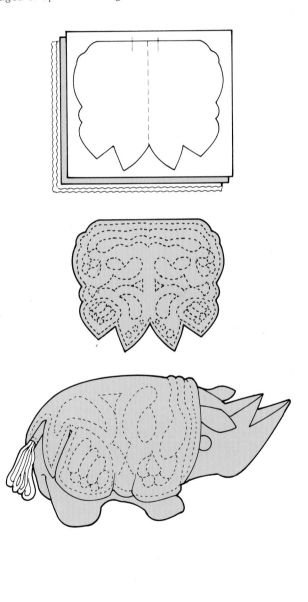

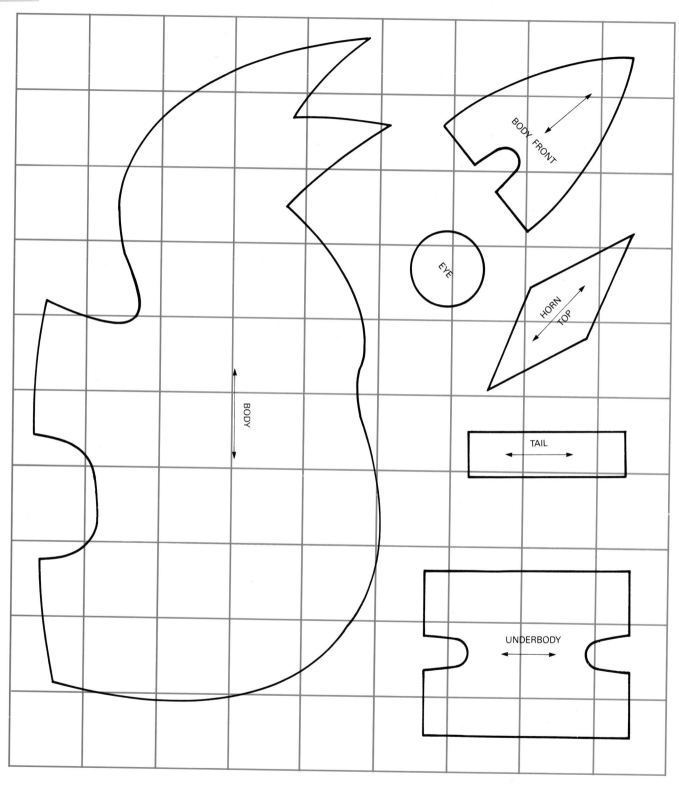

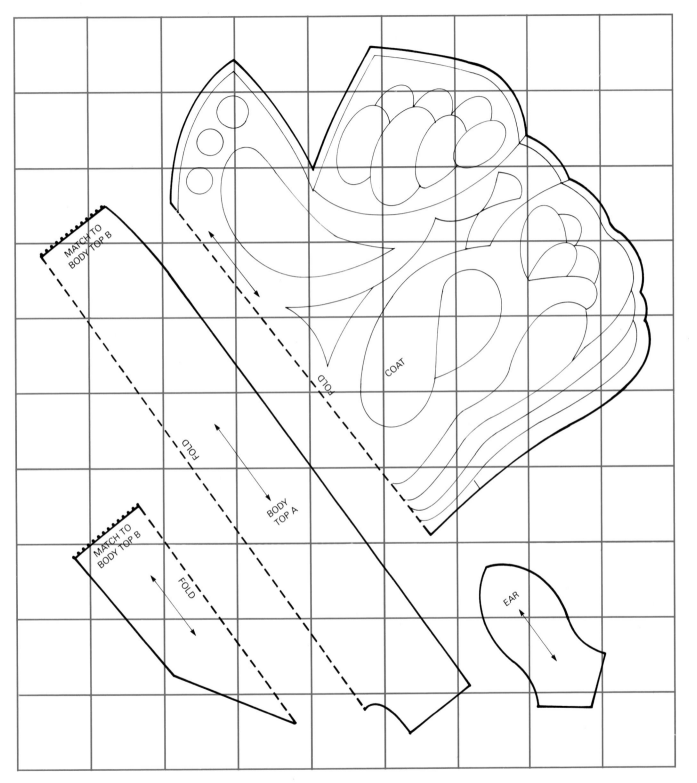

MATCH TO
BODY TOP B

MATCH TO
BODY TOP B

FOLD

FOLD

FOLD

BODY
TOP A

COAT

EAR

3
Turtle **

Almost any turtle's shell is divided into geometric sections, like a solid, three-dimensional patchwork quilt. Here, we have adapted a combination of hexagons and pentagons to give him a soft but sturdy protection.

Shell

The shell consists of turned and joined pre-quilted pieces:
2 hexagons; 2 pentagons; 6 half-hexagons.
Mark stitching lines of hexagons, pentagons and half-hexagons on wrong side of fabric, or cut templates to stitch around. Place marked fabric on facing, right sides together. Place marked fabric and facing on top of layer of wadding. Stitch through all layers, leaving opening for turning. Trim close to stitching. Clip corners. Turn inside out. Ease out corners. Hand sew opening. Topstitch close to edge and on inner quilting lines.

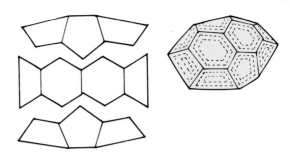

Cut a bias strip approximately the width of one hexagon and long enough to completely encircle the shell with a little overlap. Edge the entire shell with the bias strip. Pin right side of bias strip to right side of edge of shell. Stitch close to edge. Fold binding over to inside of shell. Turn raw edge in to form narrow hem. Pin hem of binding in place (binding should be wider on the inside). Handsew binding in place.

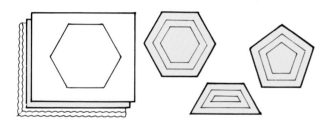

By hand, stitch edges of two hexagons together. Join half hexagons to opposite sides of joined hexagons, arranging contrasting prints as indicated. Join two half-hexagons to sides of pentagons as indicated to form sides of shell. Join sides (consisting of one pentagon and two half-hexagons) of shell to centre of shell (consisting of two hexagons and two half-hexagons).

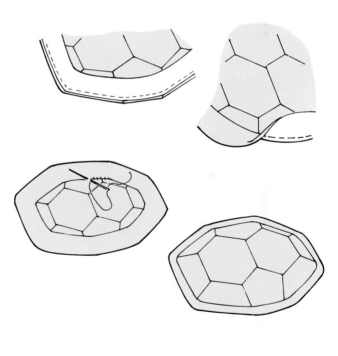

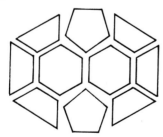

Underbody

The underbody consists of a single turned padded and quilted piece.

Mark underbody shape on wrong side of fabric or make template to stitch around. Place right sides of fabric and facing together. Place on top of wadding. Stitch through all layers, leaving opening for turning. Trim close to stitching. Clip corners and curves. Turn inside out. Ease corners out from inside. Handsew opening. Stitch close to edge and along quilting lines.

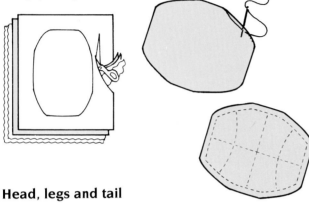

Head, legs and tail

Mark shapes of head, legs and tail on wrong side of plain fabric or make template to stitch around. Place right sides of fabric together. Place on top of wadding. Stitch through all layers, leaving opening for turning. Trim close to stitching. Clip corners and curves. Turn inside out. Ease out curves from inside. Fill head and legs with a little more wadding. Push in ends of legs to line indicated. Stitch round edges of fold to secure. Fold tail in half lengthwise. Handsew edges together.

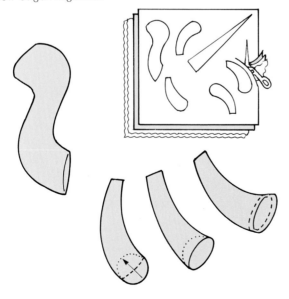

Assembly

Sew head, legs and tail to underside of shell at points indicated. Sew underbody to underside of shell, covering inner ends of legs, neck and tail. (If openings around legs, neck and tail are left wide, they can be pushed inside shell.)

Embroider eyes, or sew on beads for eyes if the toy is not to be used by very young children.

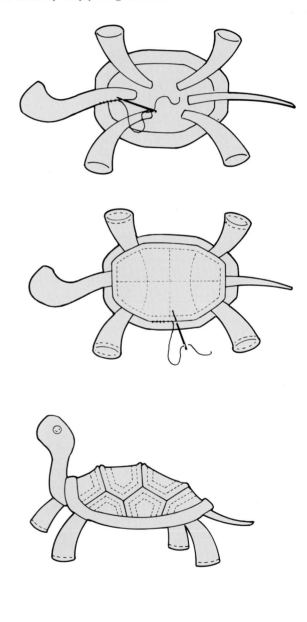

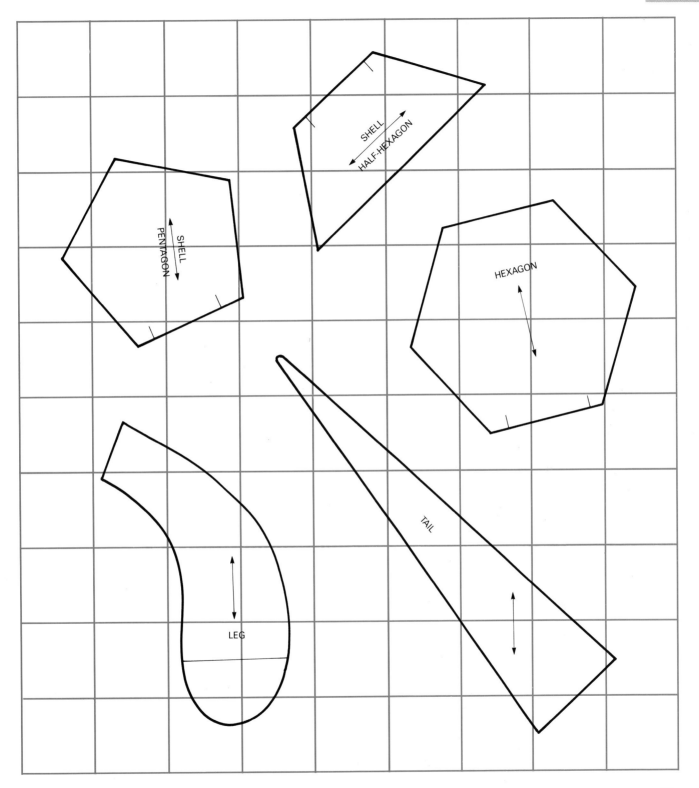

SHELL
HALF-HEXAGON

SHELL
PENTAGON

HEXAGON

LEG

TAIL

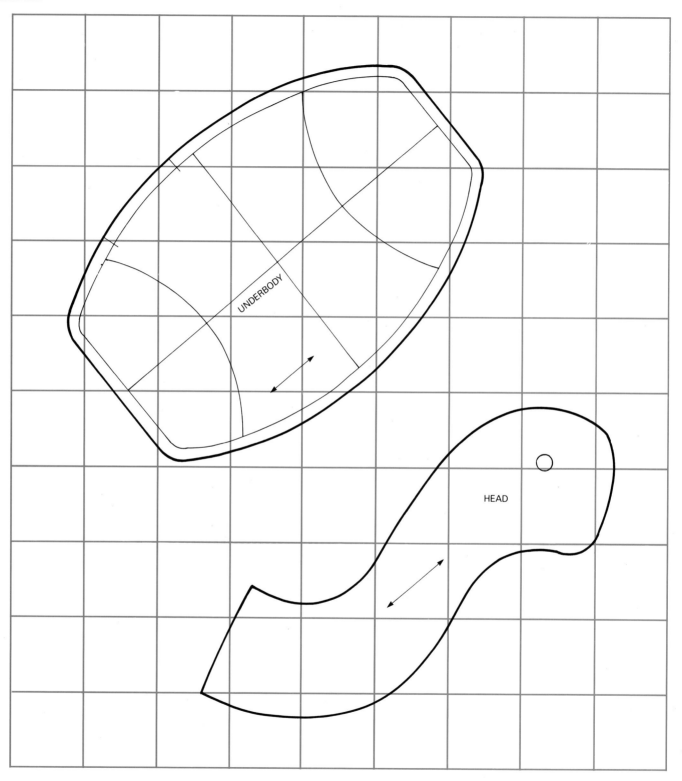

UNDERBODY

HEAD

4
Chameleon ***

With festive quilted ruff and six-colour magic coat, the chameleon changes colours with a flip of his jacket. His colour combinations can be primaries to teach colour recognition, or samples of your favourite prints.

Head

Mark head outline on right side of print fabric. Before cutting, construct eye and embroider mouth on both sides of head.

To construct the eye, mark an eye circle on piece of contrasting fabric. (See Armadillo diagram.) Cut out, leaving a narrow seam allowance. Place on a larger piece of same fabric, wrong sides together. Stitch on marked circle about three-quarters of the way round. Stuff with a little wadding. Complete stitching. Trim larger fabric to circular shape.

Mark eyes on wrong side of head piece. Draw lines dividing the circle into eight equal segments. Clip lines from the centre to the edge of the circle. Fold circle segments back on the wrong side of the fabric. Press.

Lay eye on a flat surface. Place eyehole of head over eye, centring carefully. Tack in place. Topstitch around eye on right side of fabric. Repeat with other eye.

Cut heavy paper or cardboard template of lower part of head pattern (from mouth to lower edge). Lay on right side of fabric, matching mouth and edge markings. Pin or tape in place.

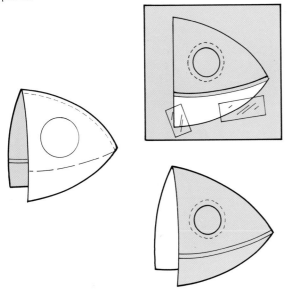

Embroider mouth by stitching a narrow zigzag satin stitch along template edge. Repeat process with other head piece.

Cut out head pieces, leaving narrow seam allowance. Place head pieces right sides together, matching eyes and edges. Stitch upper edge of head sections together.

Collar ruff

Mark collar shape on wrong side of fabric. Place on matching facing fabric, right sides together. Place both layers on a piece of wadding. Stitch through all layers, leaving curved neck edge open for turning. Trim excess fabric close to stitching and leaving narrow seam allowance around curved neck edge. Clip curves. Turn right sides out. Quilt by stitching along lines indicated on pattern.

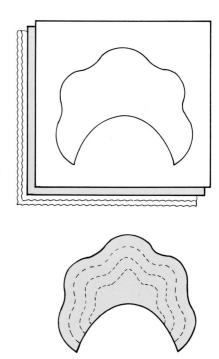

Feet

Mark four feet on wrong side of fabric. Place on matching facing fabric, right sides together. Stitch, leaving ends open for turning. Cut out feet, trimming close to stitching. Clip corners and curves. Turn right side out, easing out toe sections gently from inside. Stuff feet, but not too full. Topstitch through stuffed foot to define toes. Build in curve of feet by holding the fabric vertically while feeding it into the machine. (Be sure to change the direction of curve for two of the feet so that you have two pairs with opposing curves to fit around the body.)

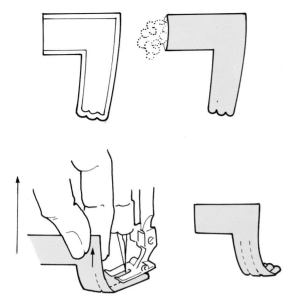

Tack remaining (rear) legs to body, right sides together.

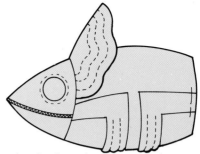

Pin tail to body, right sides together, matching point of tail base to back seam in body, right sides together, matching point of tail to back seam. Stitch. Press seam open.

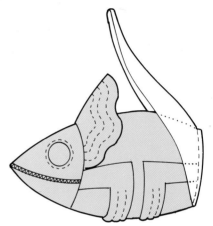

Body

Cut out body and tail, leaving narrow seam allowance. Stitch top edge of body pieces, right sides together. Arranging legs so that curve of leg follows curve of body, tack legs and collar to body as shown. Stitch head to body, catching in collar ruff and legs.

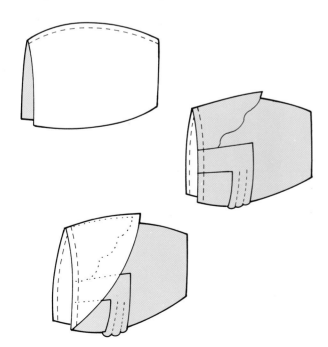

Tail, body and head will now form one continuous piece. Fold this piece in half lengthwise (along centre back seam), right sides together and matching edges. Stitch underseam of body from mouth to end of tail, leaving opening for turning.

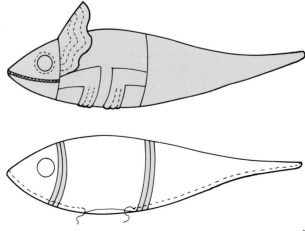

Turn right side out. Stuff, but do not stuff tail too tightly, as it will be further shaped by hand sewing. Sew opening under body.

Tail

To complete shaping of tail, put a threaded needle in at one end. Bring the needle out about 4 mm (³⁄₁₆ inch) from the end, or more if you have enlarged the pattern. Pull the thread through and work running stitch around the tail on the line indicated. Pull thread tightly to gather, forming a little ball on the end. Make a stitch to hold the thread in place. Wrap thread around tail, pulling it tightly to form a little ball on the end. Take a stitch to hold the thread in place. Put the needle in the groove formed by the wrapped thread. Push it out further along tail at next marking. Wrap to form second ball. Stitch to fasten. Repeat to base of tail. You should have a series of graduated fabric balls in a slight curve.

To curl tail tightly, run a needle threaded with strong cotton or dental floss in running stitch along seam line from end of tail to base of tail. Pull tight to curl up. Secure thread and fasten off.

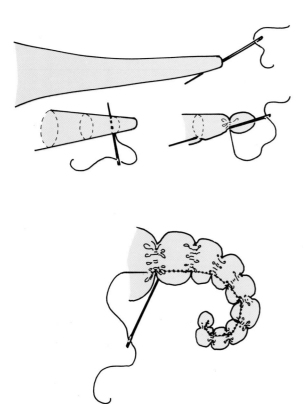

Coat

Cut two coat shapes in each of six colours of the spectrum: red, orange, yellow, green, blue and purple. With right sides together, match one coat piece to a coat piece of the adjacent colour (red and orange; orange and yellow; yellow and green; green and blue; blue and purple; purple and red). Stitch each pair along long curved side as indicated on pattern, leaving shorter curved edge open.

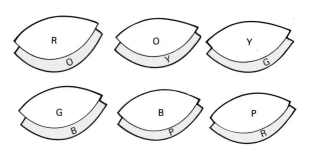

Clip curves on all pairs. Turn each stitched pair right sides out. Topstitch closed edges on all pieces, using different threads in machine and bobbin to match the different colours on each side of coat section. Leave seam allowances free to allow for joining of sections. Change machine and bobbin threads for each pair of colours, so that each surface shows matching topstitching.

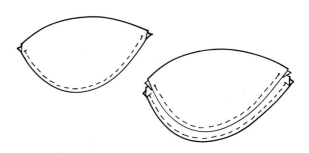

To join sections together, take the first two sections (red and orange; orange and yellow). Lay the identical colour surfaces together, matching edges. Stitch along lower edge. Repeat with all pairs but the last. You should now have a book-like form of sections with opposite colours on each side of each 'page' and two identical colours at each 'page opening'. Turn in seam allowances of last two 'pages' and sew together by hand. This will produce a closed form of six 'pages'.

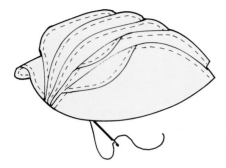

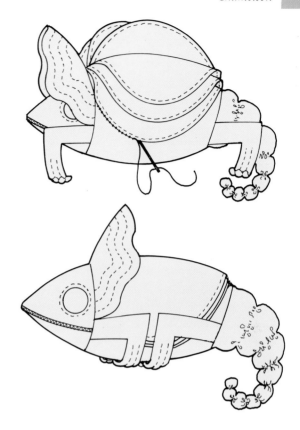

By hand or machine, quilt close to the intersection seams to hold the sides of each 'page' together. Further topstitching or quilting can be added to the sections at this point, if desired.

Turn to purple opening. Place purple surface against back of chameleon with point towards tail. Sew in place.

(**Note**: if you wish to allow the purple side to show in order to see the complete spectrum, simply cut another pair of coat shapes in the chameleon body colour, and proceed as above. In the same way, if you wish to use fewer colours, or different ones, add or subtract as you please. We chose to use the spectrum colours so that the chameleon could be used as a teaching toy, but he could change his coat to any colours you like.)

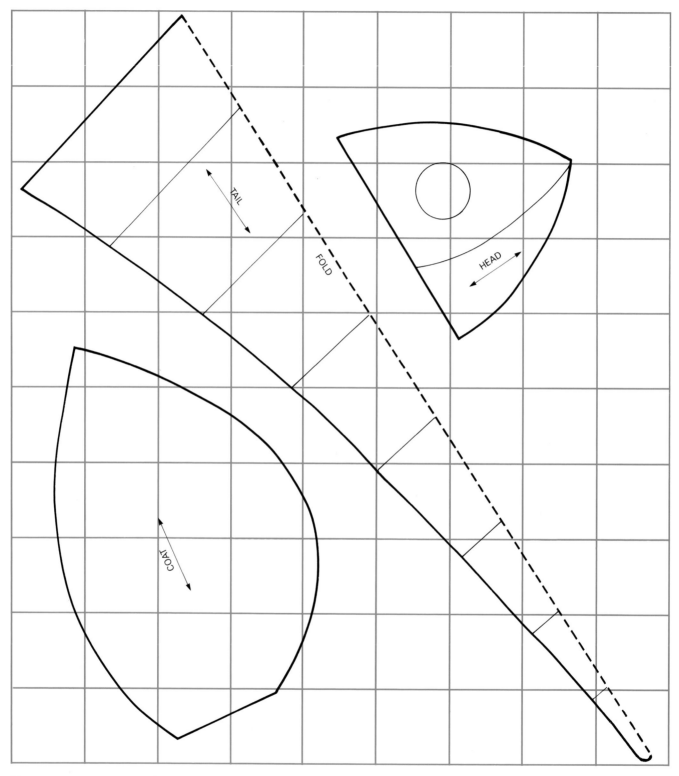

TAIL

FOLD

HEAD

COAT

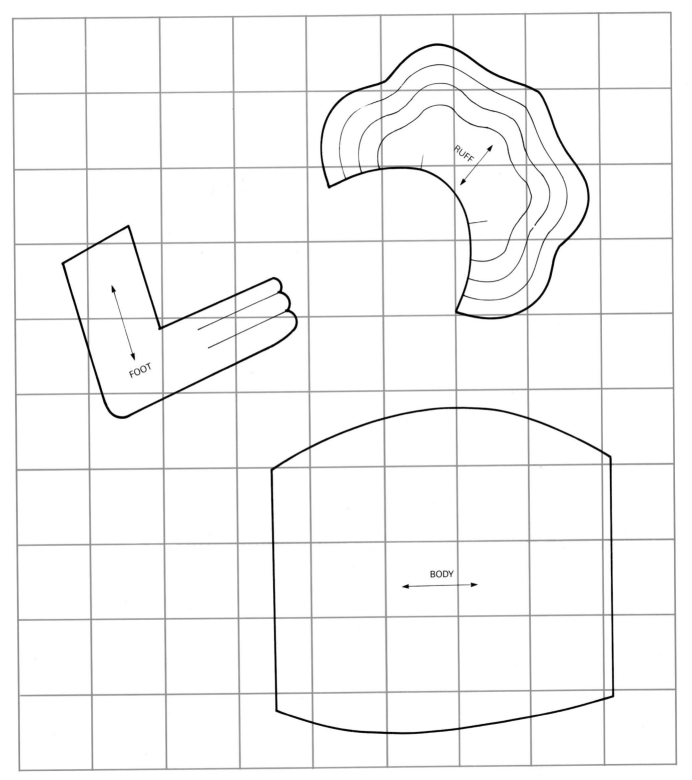

FOOT

RUFF

BODY

5
Armadillo ***

Soft underneath and well defended without, the armadillo was wearing a quilt design thousands of years ago. Instead of a coat of mail, our armadillo's coat is a pieced and quilted parka made of three or more co-ordinated fabrics.

Body

Cut larger body pieces (upper and lower body) from solid colour fabric, leaving a narrow seam allowance. Cut nose from contrasting print fabric, leaving a narrow seam allowance. For smaller pieces (feet, ears, tail) mark pattern shapes on wrong side of fabric or pin templates to wrong side of fabric. Place on another layer of the same fabric, right sides together. Stitch around all stitching lines, leaving openings for turnings.

Feet

Trim excess fabric from feet, cutting close to stitching line. Clip corners, curves and between toes, being careful not to cut through stitching. Turn right sides out, easing toes out gently from inside. Stuff the feet, beginning with the toes. (Use the blunt end of a small crochet hook to help stuff these small spaces.)

Tail

Trim excess fabric from tail, cutting close to stitching line. Clip corners, turn right sides out, and stuff, but not too tightly. To shape tail, insert needle threaded with matching cotton in one end. Bring needle out about 4 mm (⅛ inch) from the end. Wrap thread around tail and pull tightly to form a little ball on the end of the tail. Make a stitch to hold wrapping thread in place. Next, insert needle in groove formed by wrapped thread and push it out another 4 mm (⅛ inch) beyond the first groove. Wrap, fasten with a stitch, and insert needle in groove. Repeat to base of tail. You should now have a tail consisting of a series of graduated fabric beads in a slight curve or twist. (You may wish to adjust the spacing according to the size of the animal.) Tack tail to right side of one upper body piece, with base of tail aligned with edge of fabric. Place other upper body piece over the tail and the matching upper body, right sides together. (Tail will be between the two upper body pieces.) Stitch upper body pieces together along seam line.

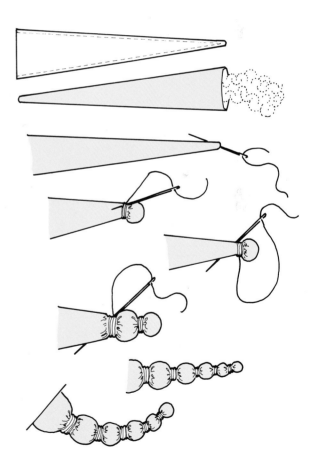

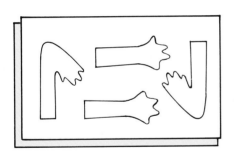

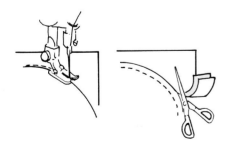

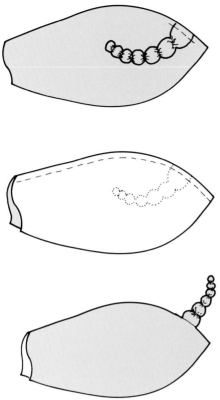

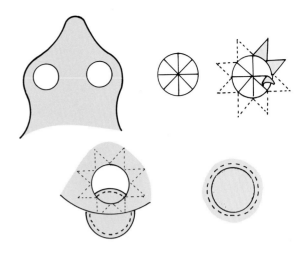

Ears

Trim excess fabric from stitched ear pieces. Clip corners and curves. Turn right side out. Press. Fold both sides in as indicated and tack in place.

Tack ears to right side of nose as shown. Stay stitch curves close to stitching line on nose and upper body. Clip to stay stitching. Tack upper body to nose, right sides together. Stitch together, catching in ears.

Eyes

To construct the eyes mark an eye circle on a piece of contrasting fabric. Cut out, leaving a narrow seam allowance. Place on a larger piece of the same fabric, wrong sides together. Stitch on a marked circle about three-quarters of the way round. Stuff with a little wadding. Complete stitching. Trim larger fabric to circular shape.

Mark eyes on wrong side of lower body. Draw lines dividing the circle into eight equal segments. Clip lines from the centre to the edge of the circle. Fold circle segments back on the wrong side of the fabric. Press.

Lay eye on flat surface. Place eyehole of head over eye, centring carefully. Tack in place. Topstitch around eye on right side of fabric. Repeat with other eye.

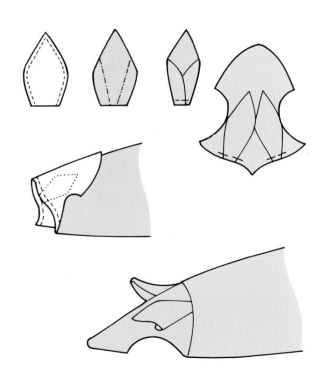

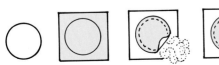

Assembly

Tack feet to right side of lower body. Tack upper body to
lower body, right sides together, matching edges and nose.
Stitch, leaving opening for turning. Trim seams where
necessary, clip curves, and turn right sides out.

Stuff body, beginning with nose. Handsew opening.

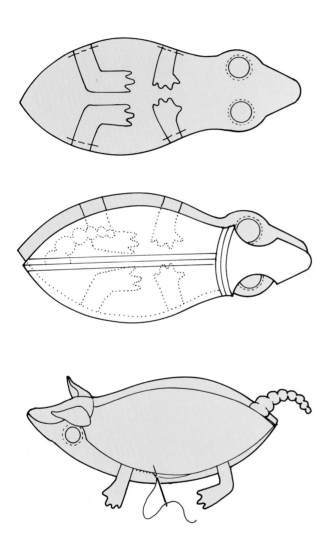

Shell

Using three or more co-ordinated fabrics and the hexagon pattern, cut 41 hexagons. Cut rectangular piece of back connecting ridge from solid fabric.

Arrange hexagons in two groups for front and rear shell as shown. To join the hexagons by machine, use a small stitch and stitch only between seam allowances (not from edge to edge). Backstitch at the beginning and end of each seam to fasten, and clip threads after sewing each seam.

To join several hexagons together by machine, follow this procedure:

1 Right sides together, stitch two hexagons together along one side (**A** to **B**). (Remember to begin and end at the corners of the stitching line and not at the edge.) Press seam. Turn over.

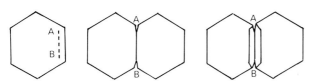

2 Add a third hexagon to the first two, placing it directly over one of the first two hexagons, right sides together. Stitch between **C** and **D**, making sure that needle stops precisely at corners of stitching line.

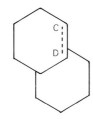

3 Leaving needle in fabric at point **D**, lift presser foot. Put point **E** on point **F** of hexagon directly underneath. Pull point **G** out as far as it will go. Pivot point **D** on needle. Stitch from point **D** to point **E**.

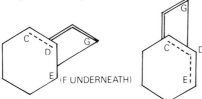

4 Press seams. Turn over to right side. Add a fourth hexagon, placing it directly over one of the three joined hexagons. Seam as before (**H** to **J**), stopping with needle in fabric at **J**.

5 Leaving needle in fabric, lift presser foot. Swing point **K** over to rest on point **L**. Pull point **M** out as far as it will go. Pivot on needle. Stitch from point **J** to point **K**.

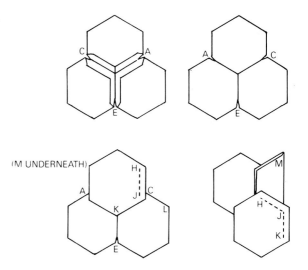

6 Press seams. Turn over to right side. Add a fifth hexagon, placing it directly over the uppermost hexagon (which will eventually be the centre of the hexagon 'flower'). Seam as before.

7 Leaving needle in fabric, lift presser foot. Swing point **N** over to rest on point **P**. Pull out point **Q** as far as it will go. Pivot on needle. Stitch to point **N**.

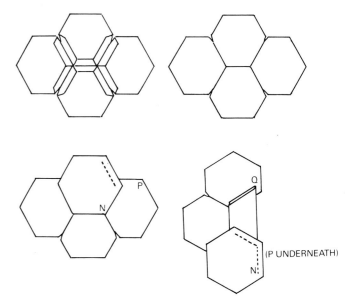

8 Press seams. Turn over to right side. Add a sixth hexagon, placing it directly over the uppermost hexagon, right sides together. Stitch to point **R**.

9 Leaving needle in fabric, lift presser foot. Swing point **S** over to rest on point **T**. Pull out point **W** as far as it will go. Pivot on needle. Continue seam between **R** and **S**.

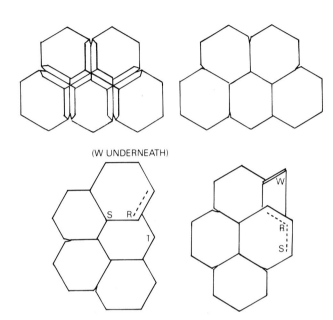

(W UNDERNEATH)

10 Press seams. Turn over to right side. Add seventh and last hexagon, placing it over last joined hexagon. Seam to point **X**.

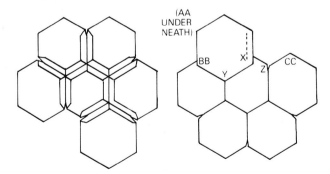

(AA UNDER NEATH)

11 Leaving needle in fabric, lift presser foot. Swing point **Y** over to rest on point **Z**. Pull out point **AA** as far as it will go and pivot on needle. Seam **X** to **Y**, leaving needle in fabric at **Y**.

12 Leaving needle in fabric, lift presser foot. Put point **BB** on point **CC**. Pivot on needle. Pull point **DD** out as far as it will go. Continue seam **Y** to **BB**.

13 Press seams. Turn over to right side. One 'flower' is completed. Add other hexagons in the same way, noticing whether you will need to sew two or three sides together for the hexagon being added.

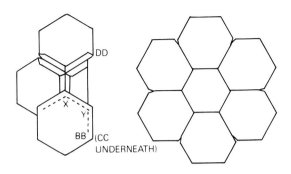

(You may of course wish to join these hexagons by handsewing. To do this, press all seams in so that no raw edges are visible: you may find this easier to do by cutting paper hexagons according to the size of your enlarged pattern and pressing the fabric around them. Then sew the edges of the hexagons together in the two groups shown above.)

Press the two completed groups of hexagons.

Place each section of shell on a piece of lining fabric, right sides together. Place both layers on a layer of wadding. Join all layers by stitching around the edges of each shell section, leaving opening for turning. Clip lining where necessary. Turn right sides out. Press. Sew opening by hand. Quilt each shell section either along seam lines ('in-the-ditch') or just inside each hexagon. Quilt by hand or machine, as you prefer.

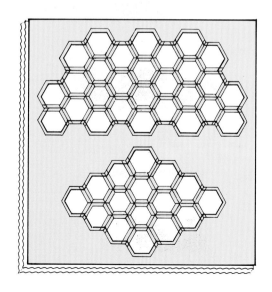

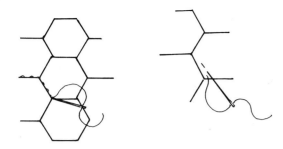

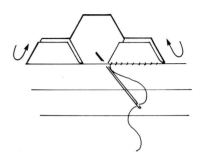

Handsew front shell section to band, leaving overlapping hexagons free. Handsew rear shell to band, starting from the middle and working out to the sides, through the centres of the hexagons. Let the band overlap the hexagons. Ease the band into a curve as you sew.

Make the ridged connecting band by placing band and facing, right sides together, on a layer of wadding. Stitch together along stitching lines, leaving opening for turning. Trim, clip corners, turn right sides out. Sew opening. Quilt along lines indicated to form a series of ridges.

Place completed quilted shell 'coat' over armadillo body. Handsew in place.

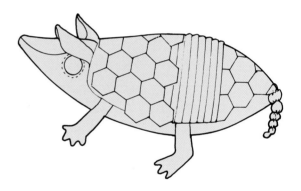

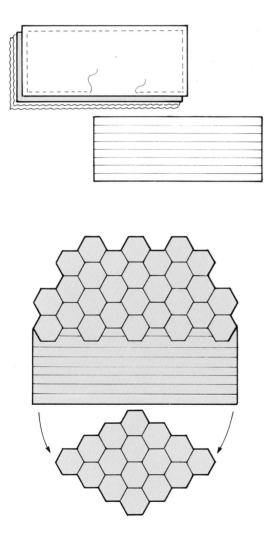

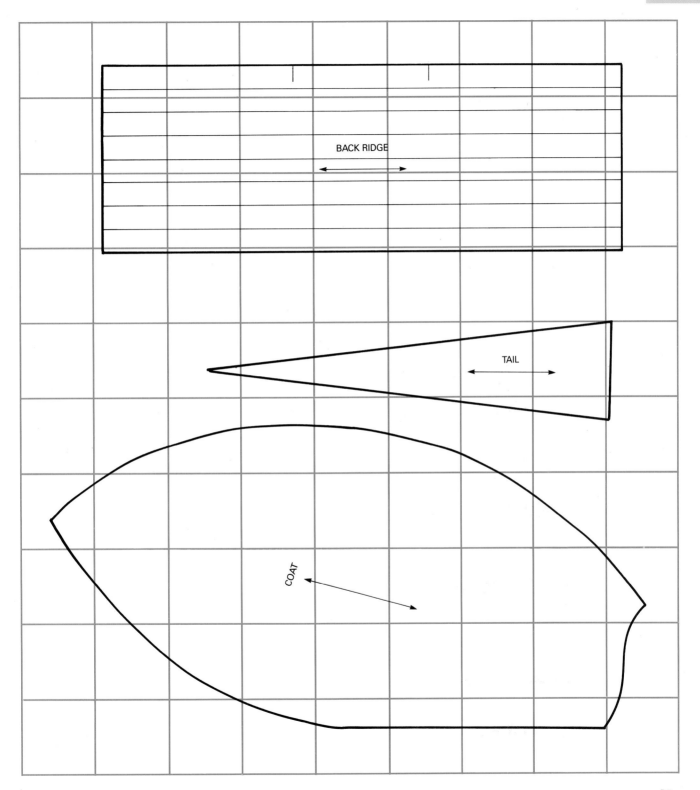

BACK RIDGE

TAIL

COAT

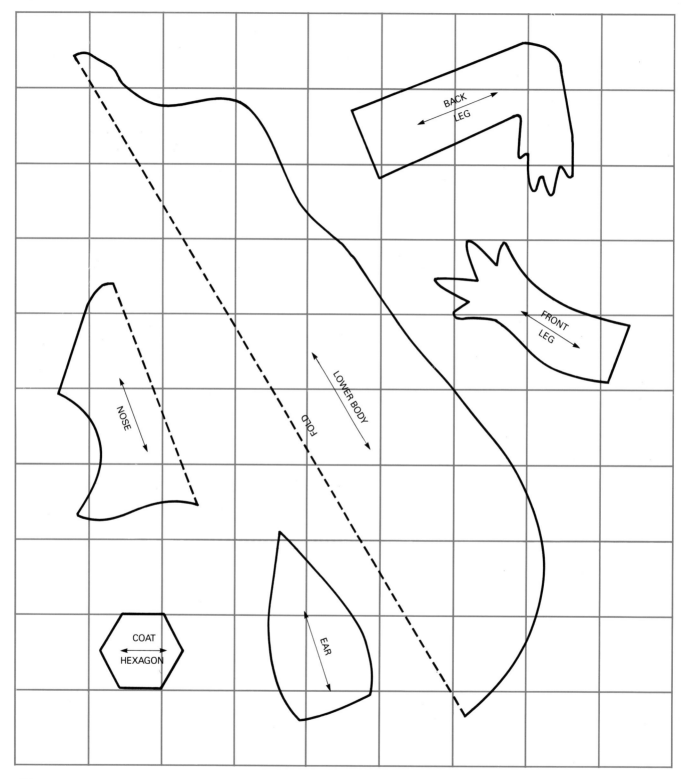

6
Bat *

This is an exceptionally quick and easy toy, made from a single pattern piece.

Mark shape of bat on wrong side of fabric or make template to stitch around. Place fabric and contrast facing, right sides together, on top of a layer of wadding.

Stitch through all layers, beginning at lower inside of leg and ending at identical point on opposite leg. Trim, making sure to leave ample seam allowance in area between legs. Clip corners and curves. Clip inner angles to stitching.

Turn right side out, easing out points on wings, nubs at top of wings, ears and feet. Handsew inside legs, leaving pointed tail section open.

Topstitch along lines above legs to define body and along fold lines on wings as indicated on pattern. (Use piece of stiff cardboard or masking tape as straight edge.) Stuff body with a little extra wadding.

Fold in seam allowance between legs, taking care to maintain the pointed shape. Handsew tail opening. Embroider eyes (or use beads if toy is not to be used by very young children). Fold ears into upright position and sew in place. Sew small pieces of velcro to feet so that bat can hang in inverted position.

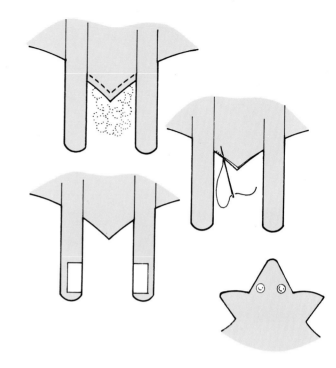

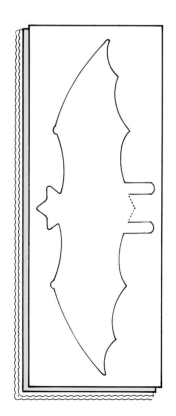

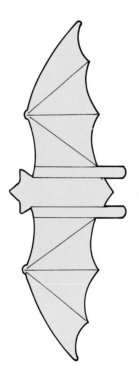

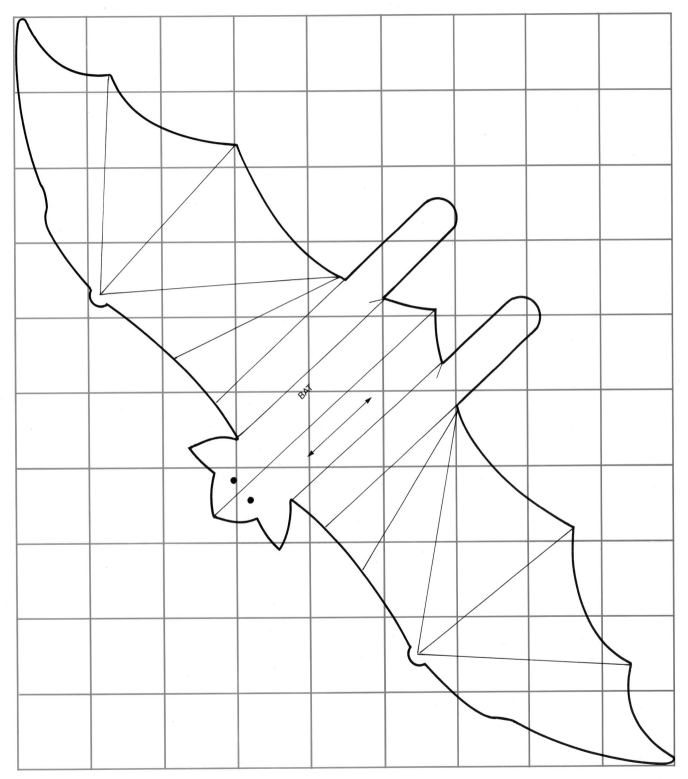

BAT

7
Stacking bunnies *

In this tiny trio, small, smaller and smallest bunnies are hollow quilted pockets that stand alone or nest inside one another.

Preparation

Prepare padded fabric for bunny body, ear and foot pieces by placing a layer of wadding between a layer of pink and a layer of white fabric (right sides out).

Using free machine sewing (drop feed, or coverplate and 0 stitch length, according to your machine), stitch randomly over the whole surface to quilt the fabric. (The more you stitch, the firmer the fabric becomes; it is important to space the stitching fairly evenly over the surface.) If you prefer, quilt by stitching in even, but fairly small-scale, geometric patterns instead of randomly.

Ears

Cut from one layer of padded fabric. Using satin stitch setting, zigzag around edges of ears, stretching very slightly as you stitch, to build curve into fabric. (The more you stretch, the more 'ruffled' the piece will become.)

Bodies

Fold the fabric with white sides together, lining side out. Mark shapes on fabric or make template to stitch around. Stitch, leaving bottom uncurved edge free and leaving opening at top of head for insertion of ears. Trim.

Insert ears inside body so that bottom edges are even with edges of body. Stitch upper edge of body, catching in ears. Zigzag or overcast curved edges to finish. Turn inside out.

Zigzag lower hem edge. Turn in to make narrow hem. Sew in place, topstitching if desired.

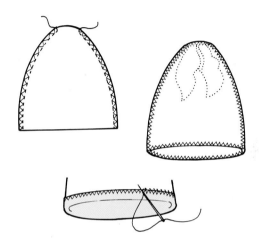

Feet

Mark shapes on pink side of prepared fabric. Fold fabric to form facing, so that white sides are together. Stitch, leaving opening for turning. Trim. Clip curves. Turn inside out. Ease shape out from inside, rolling edges gently between thumb and forefinger. (Do not press.) Handsew opening. Topstitch close to edges. To give further firmness and stability, random quilt again through all layers.

Handsew back of foot pieces to one edge of body so that body and foot form a hinge.

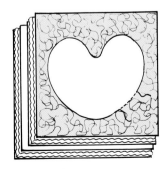
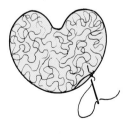

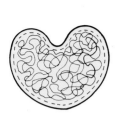

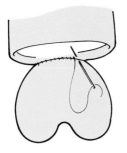

Repeat all procedures with second and third bunnies. When finished, 'stack' the bunnies by folding smallest bunny flat and folding the ears down and the feet up over the body. Place inside the middle bunny. Fold the middle bunny in the same way and place inside the largest bunny. To make bunnies stand (either stacked or singly), open out the lower edge of the hollow body shell so that it forms an open oval over the feet which form a supporting base.

Finishing

Turn bunny so that lining (pink) side of ears is up. This is the front. Embroider eyes, nose and mouth. (Beads may be used for eyes if the toy is not to be used by a small child.)

For the tail, make pompom by winding thread around a piece of card about the same width as the widest point of the ear. Tie off tightly at both ends. Tie tightly to opposite side. Cut loops. Ease out into pompom ball. Sew to lower edge of back where body meets feet.

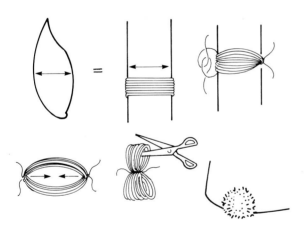

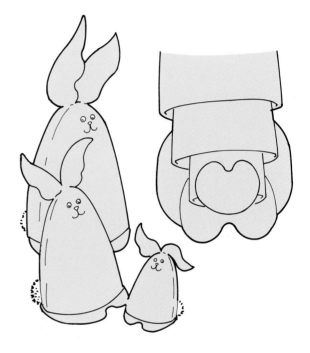

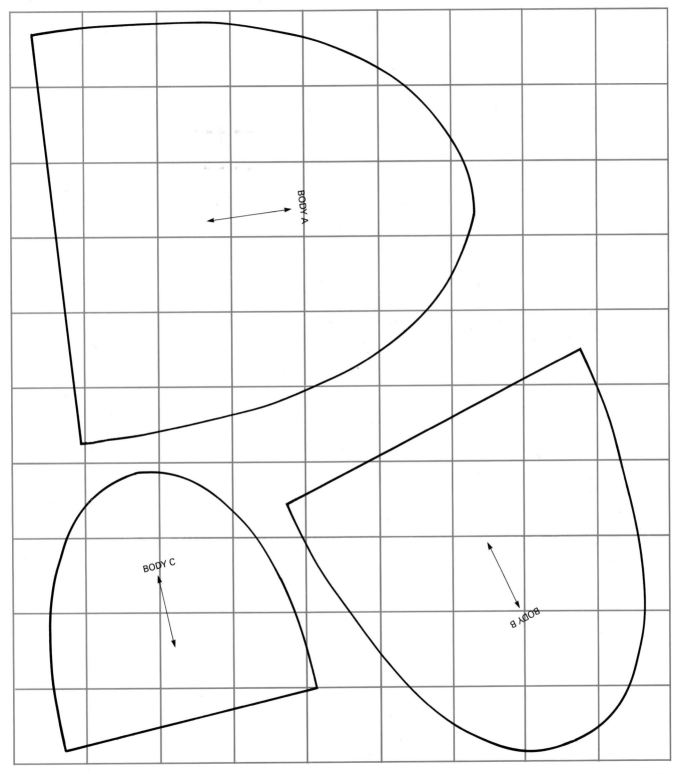

BODY A

BODY B

BODY C

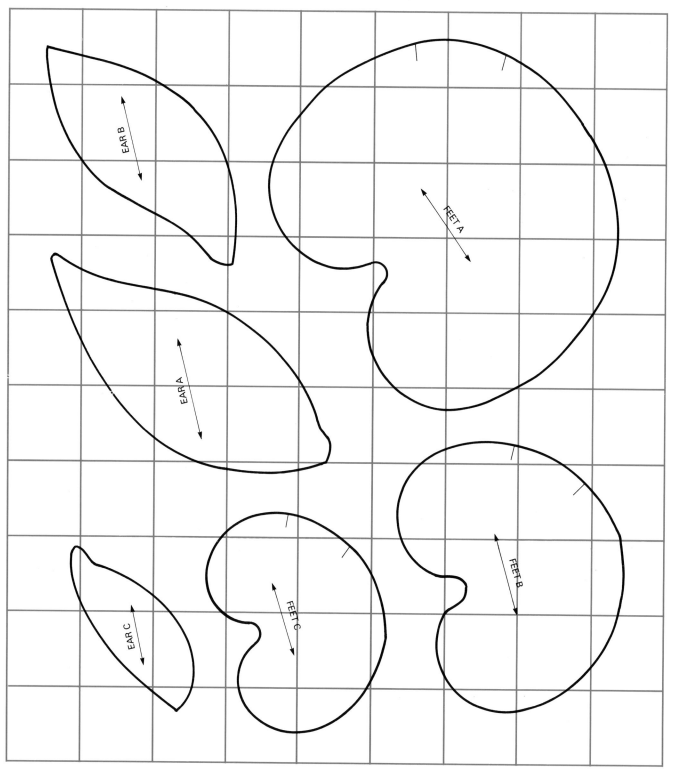

EAR B

FEET A

EAR A

EAR C

FEET C

FEET B

8
Bear *

This very simple bear's body is made from a single block which serves as a base for uneven strip or crazy patch. The block is then padded, quilted and moulded into shape with a few simple folds. Separate arms and feet are added for character and stability.

Body

Cut two body base pieces from plain fabric. On each piece, below neckline, strip patch by placing first strip over neckline, right sides together. Stitch along neckline. Turn right side over and press. Place next strip over first strip right sides together. Stitch through both layers, fastening first strip in and attaching one side of second strip. Turn right side of second strip over and press. Add third strip in the same way and continue until entire surface is covered. These strips can be any width you like, and can be placed evenly or unevenly. You could also treat this area in crazy patchwork or any other random patching method.

You now have two similar pieced rectangles. One will serve as the body. The other will provide the pre-pieced fabric for the arms and hands. (If you prefer, the two pieces can be made in one operation by starting with a plain base fabric twice the width of the body pattern and by cutting this in half to form two pieces.)

Place body on top of a layer of wadding. Quilt patched area below neckline in diagonal parallel lines as shown or in any other pattern you like.

Ears

Cut ear strips from plain body base fabric. Fold strips in half lengthwise. Stitch along seam line and across one end. Turn right sides out. Fold ear strips to form small V-shapes. Place on right side of head edge of bear body next to corner and next to centre, with 'V' pointing toward body and edges of 'V' lined up with the edge of the body base. Tack in place.

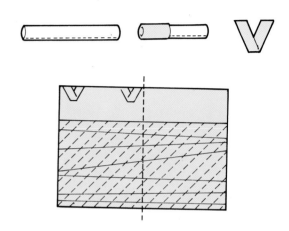

Fold body in half, right sides together, matching ends of neckline. Stitch around the three unfolded edges, leaving opening for turning. Also stitch along folded edge so that seam lines appear on both sides of the finished bear. Trim. Clip corners. Turn right sides out. Sew opening.

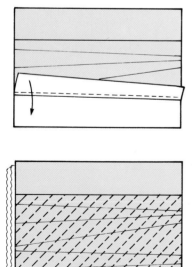

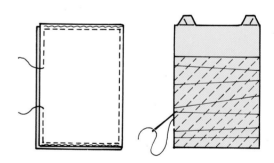

Fold bear to shape head and legs by opening out body towards the front and back, and by pushing inward toward the centre at top and bottom of body.

Bring corners of head together so that ears are close together. Shape head by making the front fold short and the back fold long and steep. The side profile should be asymmetrical.

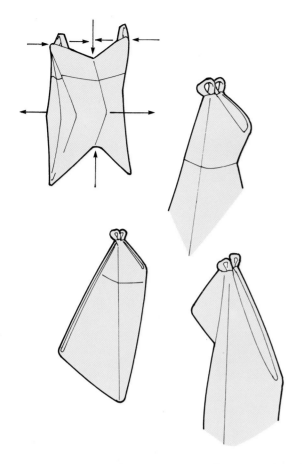

Cut circle for nose. Work running stitch along edge of nose circle. Pull to gather. Shape by gathering around small button. Press. Remove button. Fill nose with a little wadding. Pull tight and fold over end of muzzle. Sew in place.

Sew back folds of head together as far as neck to secure shape.

Arms and feet

Fold second piece of patched base fabric in half, right sides together, matching neckline edges. Place arm and hand pattern on pieced fabric so that hand falls on plain fabric and arm on pieced fabric. Mark stitching line, or use template to stitch around. Stitch, leaving end of arm open for turning. Trim. Clip curves and corners. Turn right sides out. Stuff hand with a little wadding, but leave arms fairly flat. Turn in open edges at end of arm and sew closed. Repeat with other arm.

Sew arms to sides of body at neck line, centring over side seam. Sew down back of arms a few millimetres to secure in place, leaving front of arm free.

Fold small piece of plain fabric in half, right sides together. Place on layer of wadding. Mark feet on wrong side of fabric or pin templates to stitch around. Stitch feet along seam lines, leaving opening for turning. Trim, clip and turn feet right sides out. Fill with a little extra wadding if necessary. Sew opening. Sew feet to lower corners of body, overlapping seam slightly, positioning so that feet are flat when legs are in inward folded position.

Cut necktie strip from plain fabric. Fold in half lengthwise, right sides together. Stitch along edge and across one end. Turn right sides out. Press. Tie around bear's neck and tie as necktie. Fasten tie in place at back of neck with a few stitches.

Sew front folds together to form muzzle. Sew sides of head together a little in from the folded muzzle and pull in tightly to form eye indentations and cheeks.

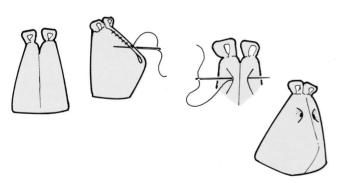

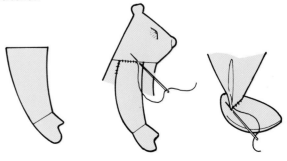

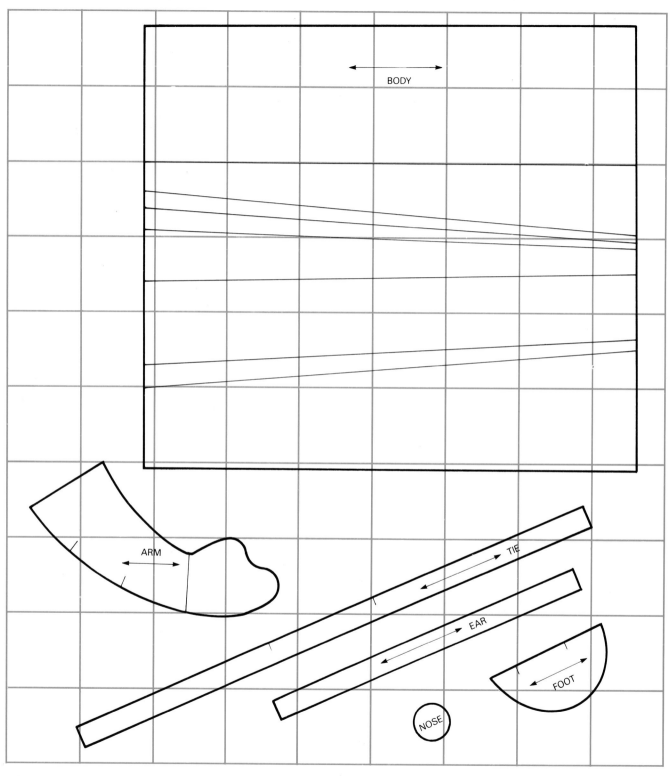

9
Badger **

Body

Piece fabric before sewing or cutting. Seam two rectangles of dark fabric to either side of narrow strip of white fabric. (For our example, we used the following measurements: dark – 255 mm × 127 mm (10 inches × 5 inches); white – 255 mm × 25 mm (10 inches × 1 inch); 6 mm (¼ inch) seams.) Press seams open.

Sew a narrow hem along one edge of a rectangle of white fabric equal in width to the pieced fabric, but half as long.

Place pieced fabric on hemmed fabric, right sides together (hem side down). Place both joined fabric and hemmed fabric on a layer of white lining fabric the same size as the pieced fabric. (Wrong side of hemmed fabric will be next to right side of lining.) Place these three layers of fabric on a layer of wadding the size of the pieced fabric.

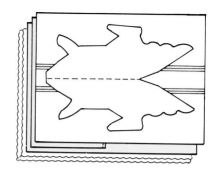

Trim. Clip corners and curves. Clip angles to seams. Pull top pieced layer away from the wadding. Place right sides of pieced layer together and stitch from back to end of tail.

Turn right side out. Pieced layer should be on top; white stripe should run along back from nose to tail. Hemmed layer forms pocket for use as puppet. Ease out head and feet. Put a little extra stuffing in legs.

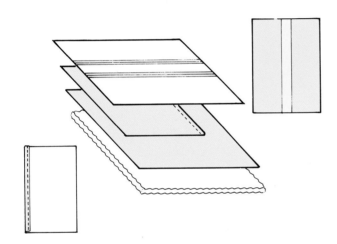

Place pattern on fabric so that fold line of pattern runs along centre of white strip. Head end should be over three layers of fabric; tail end over two layers. (White strip should be at right angles to hemmed piece.) Mark stitching line on fabric, or use pattern as template to stitch around. Stitch from nose to tip of tail. Turn pattern over. Stitch opposite side.

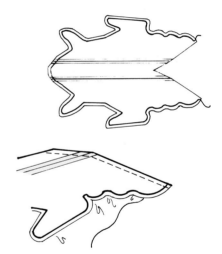

Ears and jaws

Mark circular ear shapes on wrong side of dark fabric. Place on white fabric, right sides together. Stitch, leaving opening for turning. Trim. Clip. Turn right sides out. Press. (Raw edge will be concealed under applied jaw piece.)

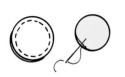

Cut two jaw pieces a little larger than pattern. Cut template or use pattern as template. Press seam allowance around template. Fold bottom edge of ear up one third of height of ear. Pin folded ear to head on each side with raw edge of opening toward nose. Place jaw pieces on edge of head as indicated, overlapping folded edge of ear. Hold in place with sellotape. Topstitch very close to edge or handsew. Remove tape.

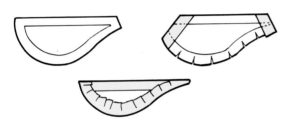

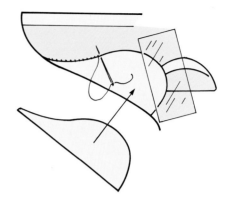

Finishing

Sew on tiny beads for eyes or, if toy is to be used for very young children, embroider eyes with two or three stitches. Handsew opening under body. Fold two sides of head together and sew in place as far as beginning of jaw.

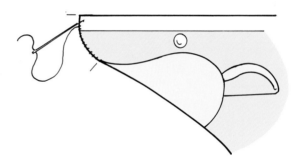

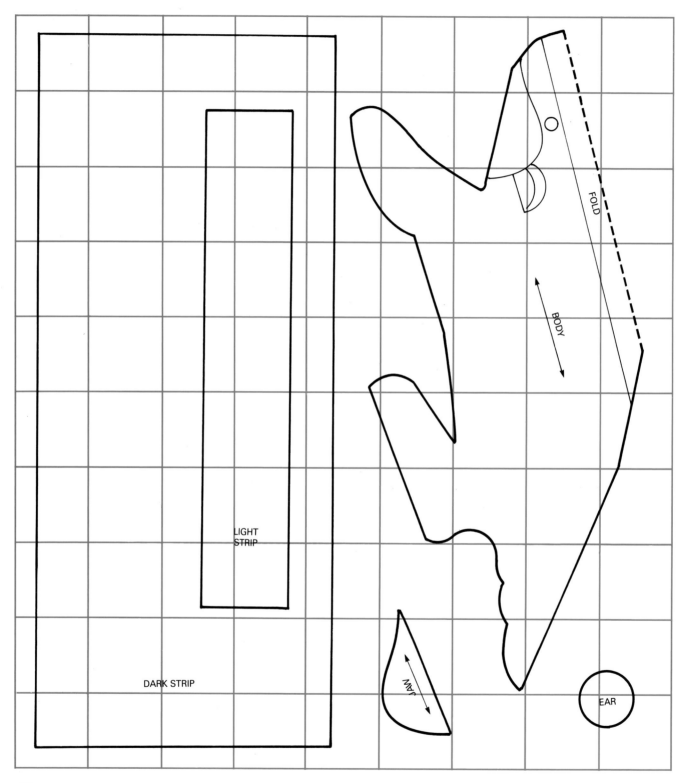

LIGHT
STRIP

DARK STRIP

FOLD

BODY

JAW

EAR

10
Chicken Littler **

Or little, littler and littlest in this soft version of a Russian stacking doll. Quilted fabric lets the birds stand alone or nest inside one another. Openings in wings let them double as hand puppets for the whole family.

Preparation

Before sewing or cutting, prepare quilted fabric by placing a layer of wadding between main and lining fabrics. Determine amount of fabric by laying enlarged pattern pieces out on fabric and allowing about 10% extra for the contraction of fabric by the quilting process. Tack layers together. Quilt by stitching through all layers in even overall pattern such as squares. (Using masking tape as a guide for sewing eliminates the need to mark the fabric.) Or, if you prefer, use purchased quilted fabric, but be sure it is reversible, with fabric on both sides.

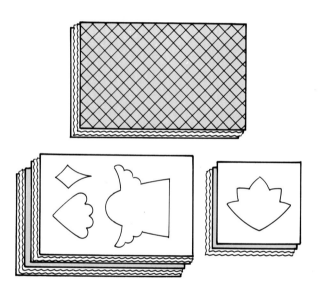

Body, bill and tail

Cut prepared fabric in half and place right sides together. Mark shapes of body, bill and tail pattern pieces on fabric, or make templates to stitch around and pin them to fabric. (We recommend stitching before cutting with small pieces. If you prefer to cut first, add a narrow seam allowance.)

Stitch around all pieces, leaving openings for turning. Trim, clip corners and inner angles. Zigzag body pieces along stitched edges and along open lower edge. Turn all pieces right sides out, easing small points out gently from inside. Sew openings in bill and tail pieces.

Turn lower open edge of body pieces in about 4 mm ($\frac{3}{16}$ inch). Tack. Topstitch hem in place. Topstitch wings

'from head, along edges, and back toward head to point marked on pattern. (This leaves an opening in the wings that allows insertion of fingers for use as hand puppet.)

Fold body in half so that side seams are touching. Crease along centre back and front. Topstitch close to edge of fold, forming small tuck to help body stand alone.

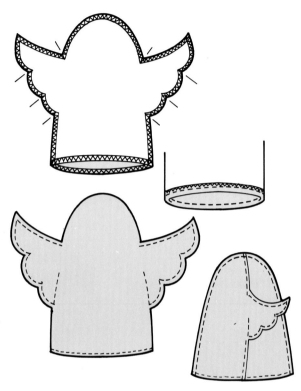

Pin bill to body, leaving lower edge free. Pinch together slightly so that bill stands a little away from body. Adjust position of sides of bill and handsew firmly in place.

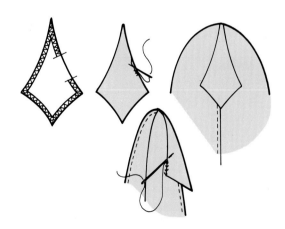

Topstitch tail close to edges and along lines joining inner points of scallops to upper point, being careful to retrace stitching exactly on 'return trips'.

To trim bill, determine length of braid required by measuring distance along edge of bill and over wing, from point of bill to centre back seam. Double this and add a few centimetres. Cut this length from purchased braid. (Or make your own by doubling a length of 4-ply yarn and zigzagging over it.) Fold the length of braid in half. Place fold at point of bill. Pin braid along edge of bill, over shoulder and across back until strands meet in centre of lower back. Sew braid to body with tiny invisible stitches. Trim excess below intersection of strands.

Feet

Place two layers of lining (or other contrast fabric) right sides together on a layer of wadding. Mark stitching lines of foot shapes or pin templates to fabric. Stitch through all layers, leaving opening for turning. Trim excess fabric. Clip corners and between toes, being careful not to cut the stitching. Turn right sides out, easing out points gently from inside. Topstitch around edges, leaving opening free. Add a little more stuffing to padded feet. Sew opening. Complete topstitching along sewn opening. Topstitch in centre of foot from upper point to lower point, forming two feet.

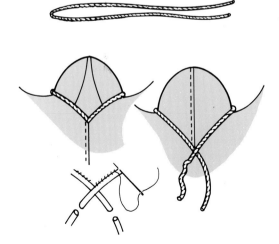

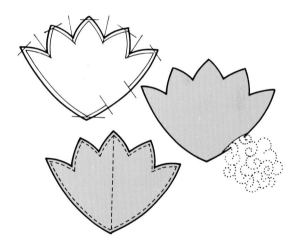

Pin tail to body back, letting point just cover intersection of braid ends. Sew by hand to body between circles. Fold tail up along line between circles and sew to body along fold, hiding ends of braid.

Match point of feet to tuck in centre back of body. Sew edges of feet to back lower edge of body. Sew only about half-way to side seams, to allow body to open out over feet. Reinforce at outer edges by taking several extra stitches before fastening off.

Spread body out over feet to allow Chicken Littler to stand. On largest bird, sew button in channel between feet. Work button loop at centre front hem.

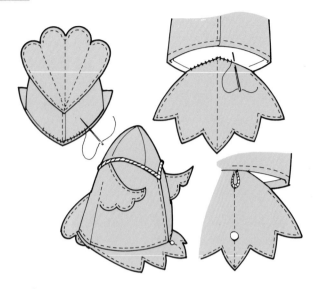

Repeat all procedures for two smaller birds. Fit together by folding wings of smallest bird in and folding feet up, flattening body. Fold feet away from body of middle bird, and slip folded littlest bird inside body of middle bird. Repeat, fitting middle bird inside largest bird.

Finishing

Form loop of braid (like braid trim on bill) from a length about eight times the distance from top of head to point of bill. Sew ends of braid together to form a single loop. Form 'feathers' by dividing loop into two loops and then dividing each loop again to make four. Sew securely together at centre point of contact. Lay loops flat in a fan-shape, so that the sides of the loops are touching. Sew two centre loops together from point to about 12 mm (½ inch) from point. Repeat, joining inner and outer loops.

Sew 'feathers' to top of head. Sew pearl beads close to top of head on sides of bill. (Embroider eyes if to be used by small children.)

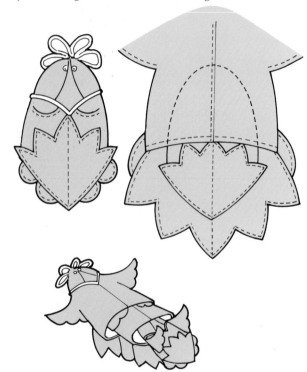

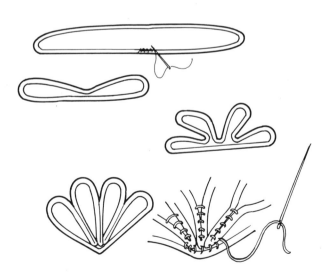

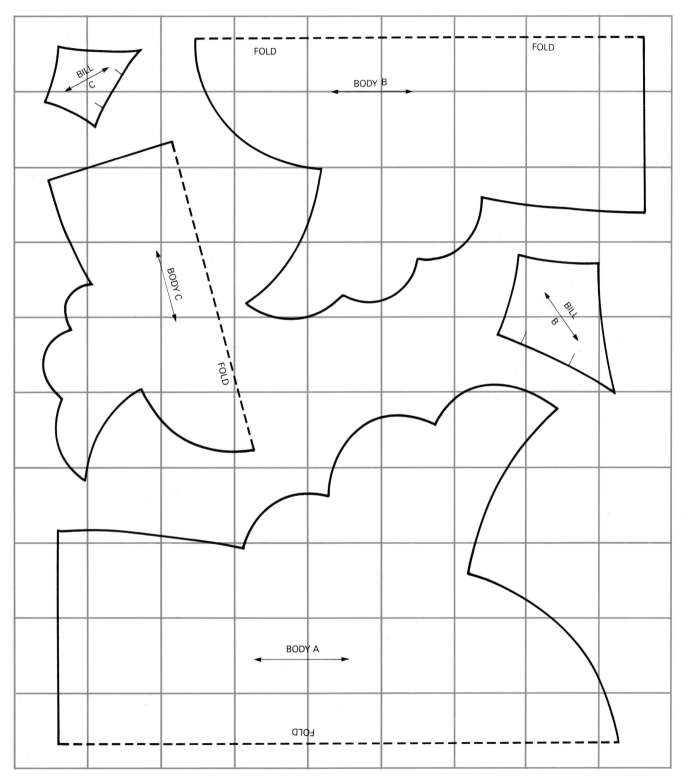

FEET A

TAIL B

TAIL A

FOLD

FEET B

BILL A

FEET C

FOLD

TAIL C

11
Frog prince mask ***

This mask is a frog that really does turn into a prince. It consists of two joined padded head pieces and a padded crown/collar. It can be made small to fit a doll or large enough for a child. To determine size, measure the head of the wearer at its widest point (include nose!). Add 8 cm (3 inches) to measurement; divide in half. This should be measurement of widest point of enlarged pattern of face. Be sure to check the eye placement of enlarged pattern so that pupils of frogs eyes fall over eyes of wearer. Adjust pattern as necessary

The frog and prince faces are made separately, then joined.

Prince face

Mark shapes of face and features on right side of face fabric. With right sides up, pin fabric to a layer of wadding. Stitch features: satin-stitch eyebrows, nose, moustache and mouth. Mark, but do not stitch, eyes. Cut small circles of pink fabric for rosy cheeks; pin in place; satin-stitch to secure. Fill nose with a little extra wadding so that it projects slightly. Zigzag around outer edge of face to secure to wadding, taking care not to stretch the shape.

Frog face

Mark shape of face and position of eyes on right side of green fabric. Cut eye circles; pin in position. Zigzag satin stitch round *outsides of eyes only*. (Pupils will be made later as openings through the joined faces.) Zigzag around outer edge of face.

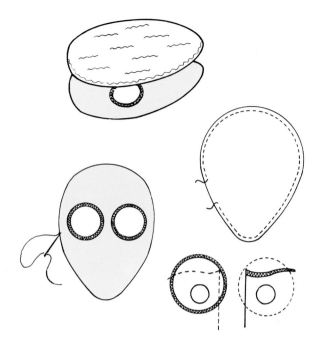

Head back

Mark shape of head back on wrong side of green fabric (or make template to stitch around). Place right sides of brown and green fabric together. Place on top of wadding. Stitch through all layers, leaving opening for turning. Trim. Clip corners and curves. Turn inside out. Ease out edges from inside (do not press). Handsew opening. To quilt, tack layers together to prevent puckering. Stitch along indicated lines through all layers of turned padded piece.

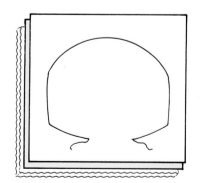

Joining faces

Trim face pieces, leaving at least 8 mm (¼ inch) seam allowance beyond stitching line. Place right sides together, making sure that prince's eyes fall well within the white circles of the frog's eyes. Stitch around outer edge, leaving opening for turning. Clip curve. Turn face right side out. Ease edges out from inside, defining edges by rolling gently between thumb and forefinger. (Do not press). Handsew opening.

Zigzag around prince's eyes with close setting. (This operation will go through both layers, and if correctly placed, eye circles will fall within the white circles on the frog side; check position before sewing.) Cut out centres of eyes close to stitching through all layers. Trim carefully. Zigzag around eye ring again to give finished edges on both sides.

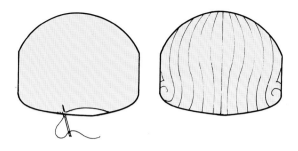

To form crown openings for eyes (in frog position, when base of crown is underneath frog face), zigzag around two centre squares at bottom of crown. Cut out centres of squares and zigzag again to finish edges. (Check position of openings before stitching, especially if you have changed the eye position on face; eye openings in crown should coincide exactly with the frog eye openings when mask is in frog position if correctly spaced.)

Form crown shape by matching the two short edges of the crown. Slip-stitch together invisibly.

Crown

Mark shape of crown on wrong side of fabric (or cut template to stitch around). Place fabric and facing with right sides together on top of layer of wadding. Stitch through all layers, leaving opening for turning. Trim close to stitching. Clip corners to inner points of stitching. Turn right sides out. Ease out edges and points from inside with knitting needle. Quilt by stitching along indicated lines.

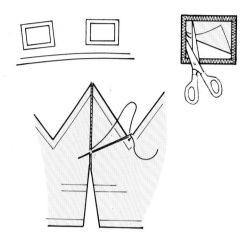

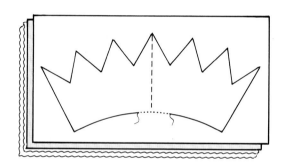

Assembly

Place green sides of face and head back together. Sew face and head back together by hand or machine zigzag as far as lower edges of eyes.

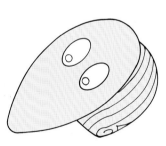
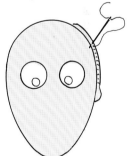

Slip crown over prince head so that square openings in crown are positioned directly above eyes. Make sure that the distance from the edge of the crown to the centre of each open square is exactly the same as the distance from the edge of the crown to the centre of the eyes. This will position the eye holes correctly when crown is folded down in frog position.

Pin. Hand sew in place.

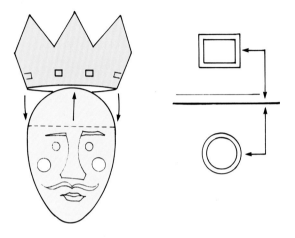

Turn to frog side by pulling the green side down and over the crown while pushing the centre of the head up from the inside.

(**Note** If you are making this for a doll rather than a child, the eye openings and the square openings in the crown may be omitted.)

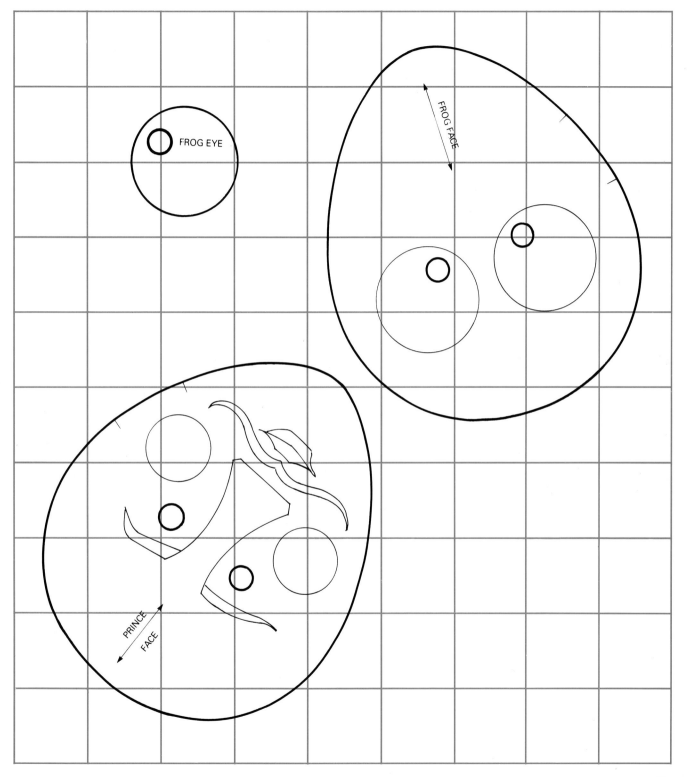

FROG EYE

FROG FACE

PRINCE FACE

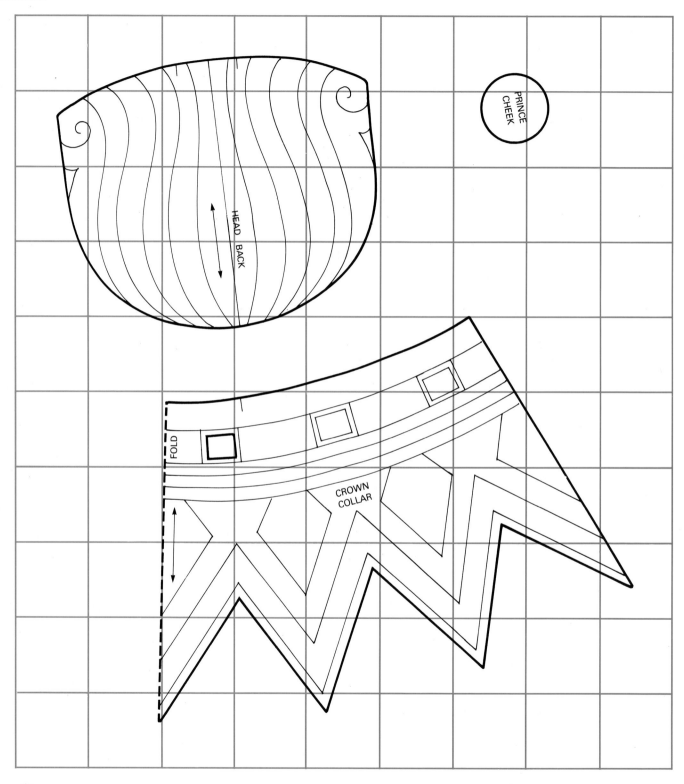

PRINCE CHEEK

HEAD BACK

FOLD

CROWN COLLAR

12
Shape-matching book ***

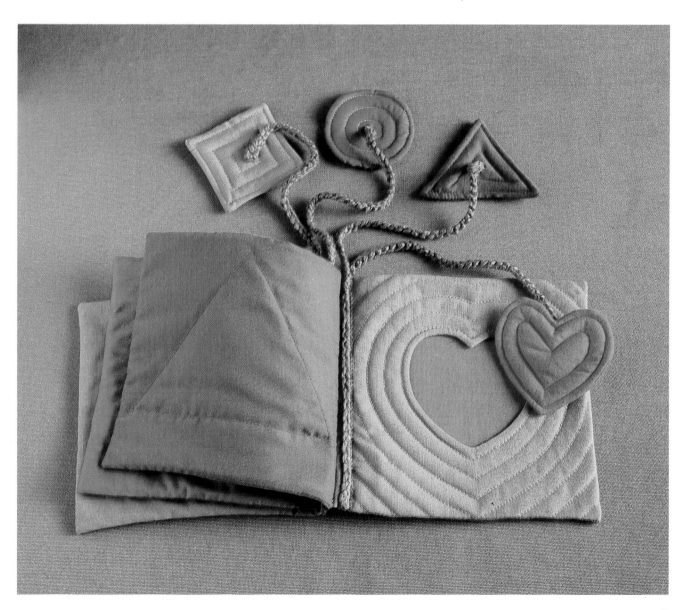

This consists of four square lined and quilted pieces bound together in a book. Each page has a different shaped opening and pocket in the centre. Matching shapes are attached by cords and give early learning practice in colour matching and shape recognition.

Pages

Choose a different colour for each page. Use the colour of the previous page for the lining of each page. For example, use the heart page colour for the square page lining, the square page colour for the circle page lining and so on. The separate colour shapes will match the linings of the corresponding pages; the lining colour appears as the shape colour through the shaped page opening.

Place right sides of fabric and facing together. Place on top of a layer of wadding. Mark shapes on wrong sides of fabric or make template to sew round. Stitch *centre shapes only* through all layers. Trim *inside* shapes close to stitching. Clip corners or curves. Turn facing to underside. Pin edges of fabric, batting and facing together. Stitch close to opening and again at regular intervals following centre shape as indicated.

Place right side of lining next to right side of shape page. Mark edge of page on wrong side of lining fabric. Tack. Stitch from page side to keep stitching straight and in line with stitching on page. Trim. Clip corners. Turn inside out through cut-out 'window'. Work out edges and corners. Stitch through both page and lining along one of the quilting lines near third row from centre to form pocket around centre for holding shape. Repeat for all four pages.

Binding strip

Stitch binding strip to facing, leaving opening for turning. Trim; clip corners. Turn inside out. Work out corners from inside. Press. Sew opening. Stitch pages with zigzag or overcast to binding strip, beginning with outside pages, square and heart. Then insert circle and triangle pages as the second and third pages.

Shapes

Mark shapes on wrong sides of fabric or cut templates to stitch around. With right sides together, place fabric and facing on top of layer of wadding. Stitch through all layers, leaving opening for turning. Trim; clip corners or curves. Turn inside out. Handsew opening, being careful to maintain shape. Topstitch close to edge. Quilt by topstitching at regular intervals between edge and centre.

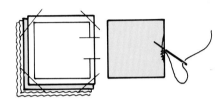

Cords

Make two cords. Cut two bias (cross) strips, the same colour as binding, each four times height of book. Fold lengthwise. Stitch along edges and one end. Turn right sides out. Turn in raw edge and sew folded edges together. (If you prefer, use cords made of zigzagged doubled lengths of yarn instead of bias strips.) Fasten one end of cord to centre of one shape by oversewing firmly. Fasten other end to centre of second shape. Repeat with second cord and remaining two shapes.

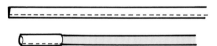

Assembly

Open first page of book. Position cords: with first shape at top, lay cord along inside binding strip. Turn page. Fold cord at bottom and lay along binding so that both shapes are at top. Zigzag or handsew to secure. Repeat with second cord and next two openings of book.

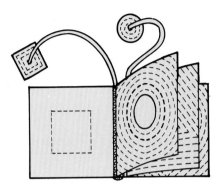

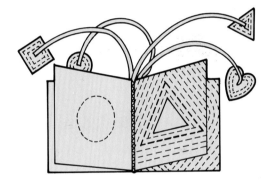

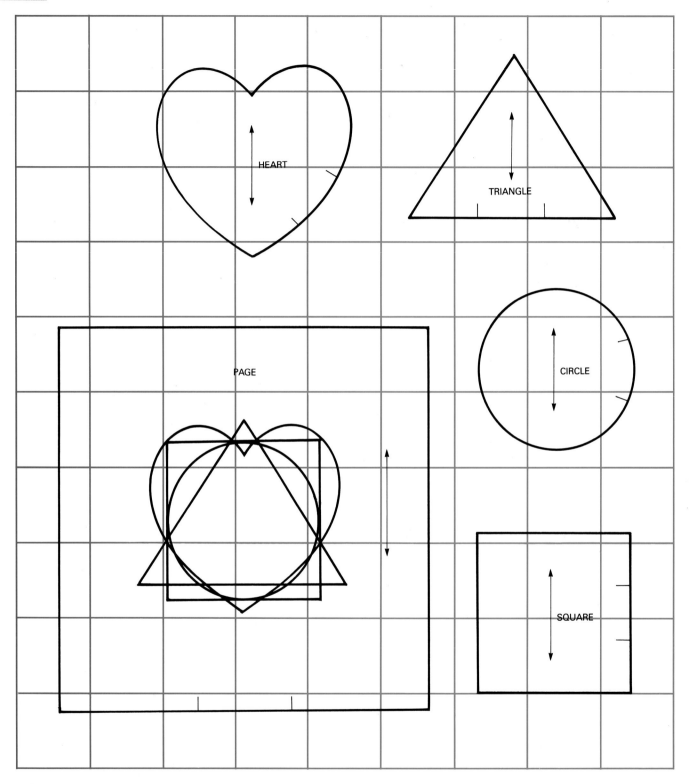

HEART

TRIANGLE

CIRCLE

PAGE

SQUARE

13
Bird purse ***

For compactness, only the wings, feet and feathers of this folding bird purse are padded. But the variety of piecing offers the opportunity to use a quilter's scrapbag to good effect.

Body back

With right sides together, place body back fabric on body back facing fabric. Mark body back and inside wing pockets on fabric or cut templates to stitch around. Stitch, leaving openings for turning. Trim. Clip corners and curves. Turn right sides out. Press.

Tack inside wing pockets to lower edges of wings. Overcast to edges. Stitch through all layers along feather lines. Stuff openings from inside body back with a little wadding. (Use small knitting needle to push filling into small spaces, a little at a time.) Handsew opening.

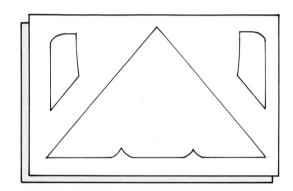

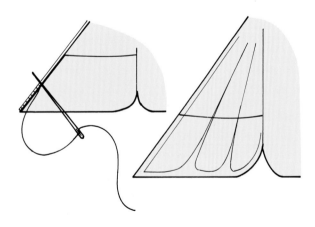

Body front

Place body front fabric to facing fabric, right sides together. Mark shape or pin template to fabric. Stitch, leaving opening for turning. Trim. Clip corners and curves. Turn right sides out. Ease out edges and points from inside. Press. Handsew opening.

Repeat with front pocket. Pin front pocket to body front as indicated. Fasten together by topstitching through all layers along sides and lower edge of pocket.

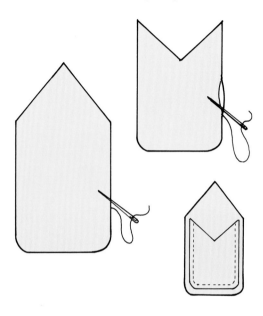

Back pocket

The back pocket is like a little backpack, consisting of two pieces: a back piece with a flap and a shorter front piece.

With right sides together, place pocket back fabric on contrasting facing. Mark shape. Stitch, leaving opening for turning. Trim. Clip. Turn right sides out. Press.

For other side of back pocket, piece two contrasting pieces together. Press seam open. Place pieced fabric on facing with right sides together. Mark shape, using lower section of back pocket pattern, eliminating upper curve. Stitch, leaving opening for turning. Trim. Clip. Turn right sides out. Press.

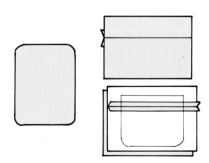

Place longer side of back pocket in position on body back. Place shorter, pieced side of back pocket over longer side, matching lower edges exactly. Pin. Tack. Topstitch sides and lower edge to body back through all layers, leaving flap at top free to fold over front pocket.

Feathers

Mark shape on right side of fabric. Appliqué smaller pieces of contrast fabric to feathers. Place layer of wadding between fabric and lining, right sides out. Zigzag around shape. Trim. Satin-stitch around edge, stretching a little as you stitch to give a slightly ruffled effect. Stitch lengthwise along centre of each feather.

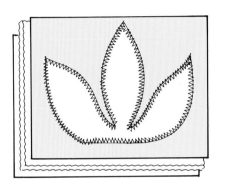

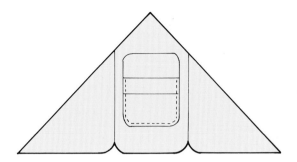

Feet

Mark shape on wrong side of fabric or cut template to sew around. With right sides together, stitch feet to facing, leaving upper edge open for turning. Trim. Clip corners and points. Turn right sides out. Ease out points from inside. Fill toes with a little wadding, working it down into the points. Use just enough to pad slightly; do not fill too full.

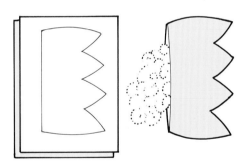

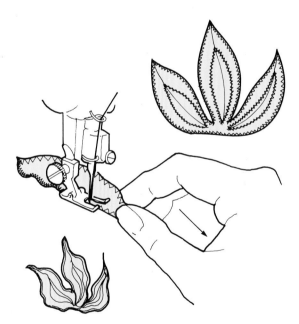

Assembly

Tack feet to inside lower edge of body back. Pin body front to body back, covering upper edge of feet. Topstitch sides and lower edge of body front, fastening in feet by stitching through all layers.

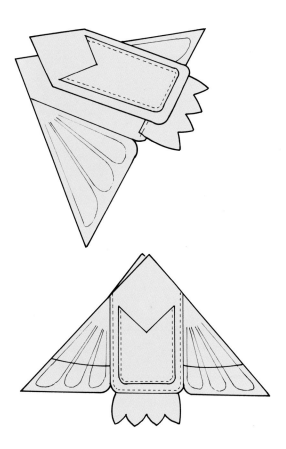

Fold triangular top edge over to form bird's head. Sew feathers to top of head. Embroider eyes (beads may be used if not for very young children). Sew press fasteners to inside tip of outer wing and near curve on outside of inner wing, so that the wings can be fastened in a closed position.

For the cord, cut narrow bias strip about six times the height of the bird body. Fold lengthwise, right sides together. Stitch through both layers along long edge, leaving ends open for turning. Turn right side out. Stitch ends together to form long loop. Pin one end of loop around lower edge of rear pocket and to top of body back as far as pocket fold. Handsew around edge. (The portion of cord around pocket flaps may be left free as belt loop.)

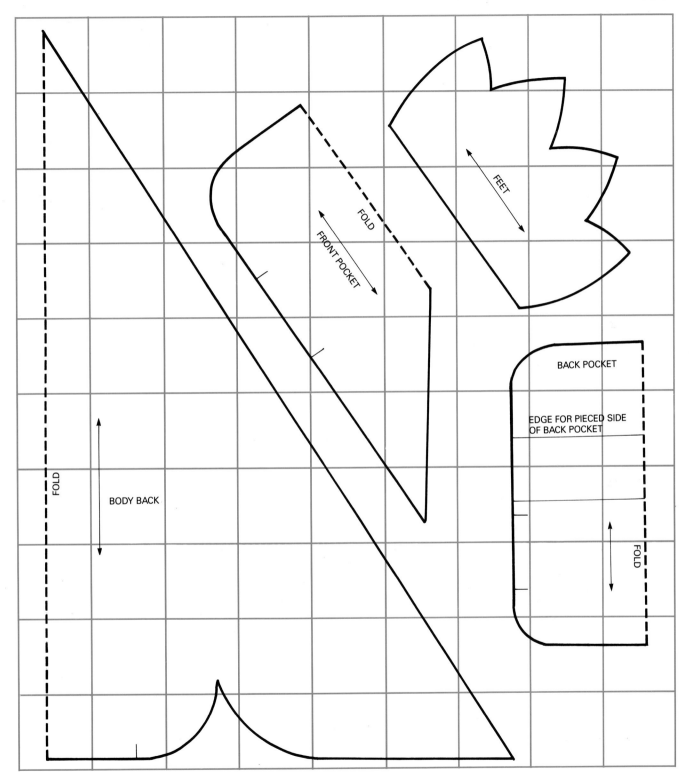

FEET

FOLD

FRONT POCKET

BACK POCKET

EDGE FOR PIECED SIDE
OF BACK POCKET

FOLD

FOLD

BODY BACK

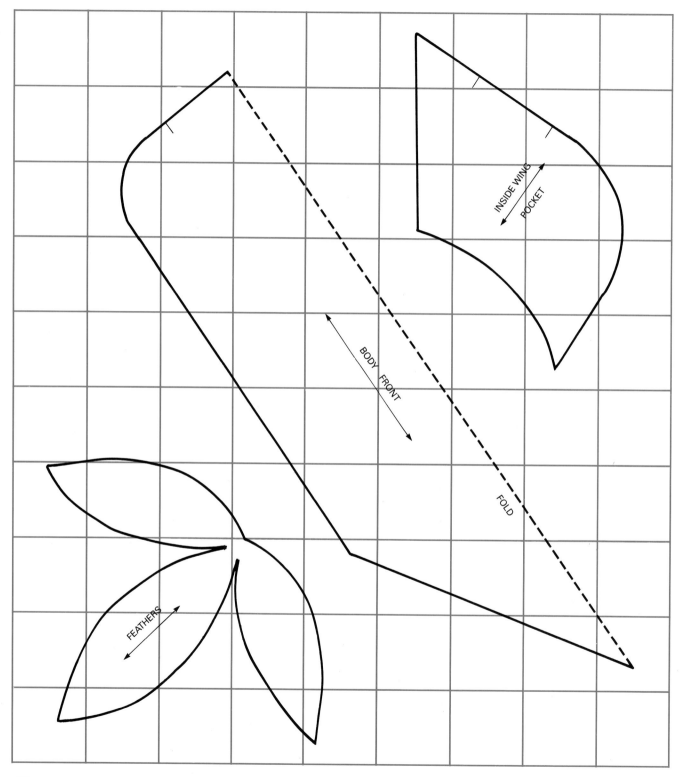

INSIDE WING

POCKET

BODY FRONT

FOLD

FEATHERS

14
Dragon shoes *

These funny three-toed slippers are made from a single pattern piece, padded, curved and stitched into shape. Make them small for a doll or life-size for a child who can practice lacing and tying.

Shoes

Enlarge or reduce pattern as desired. To fit a child's foot, draw an outline of the foot. The outline should fit well within the centre point of the central trefoil. Enlarge accordingly.

Mark shoe pattern shape twice on wrong side of fabric or cut template to stitch around. Place fabric on lining, right sides together. Place both layers on a layer of wadding. Stitch through all layers, leaving opening for turning on long straight edge. Stitch again close to first stitching to reinforce corners and points. Trim excess fabric. Clip corners, angles and curves. Turn right sides out, easing out points gently from inside. Handsew opening.

Topstitch 2 mm ($\frac{1}{16}$ inch) from edge. Quilt by stitching at regular intervals parallel to edges and on centre trefoil, as shown.

To form shoes, bring outer points **A** to centre point **C**, matching inner toes **B**. Handsew 'uppers' together about 8 mm ($\frac{3}{8}$ inch) toward opening. Handsew upper shoe to 'sole' by sewing inner two layers together.

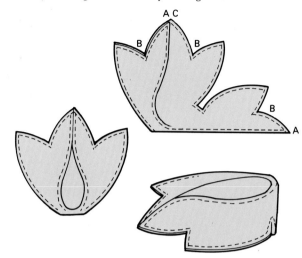

Eyelets

Using purchased eyelet tool, attach four metal eyelets to each shoe, following instructions on package. (If toy is to be used by a very young child, eyelets should be worked by hand.) Thread purchased shoelaces through eyelets. Tie in bow.

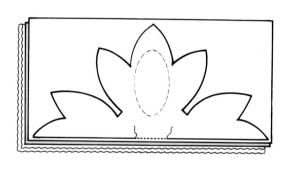

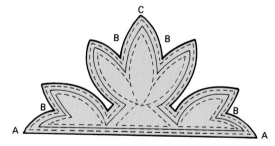

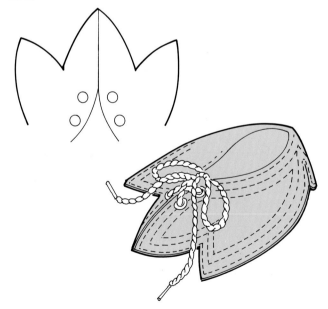

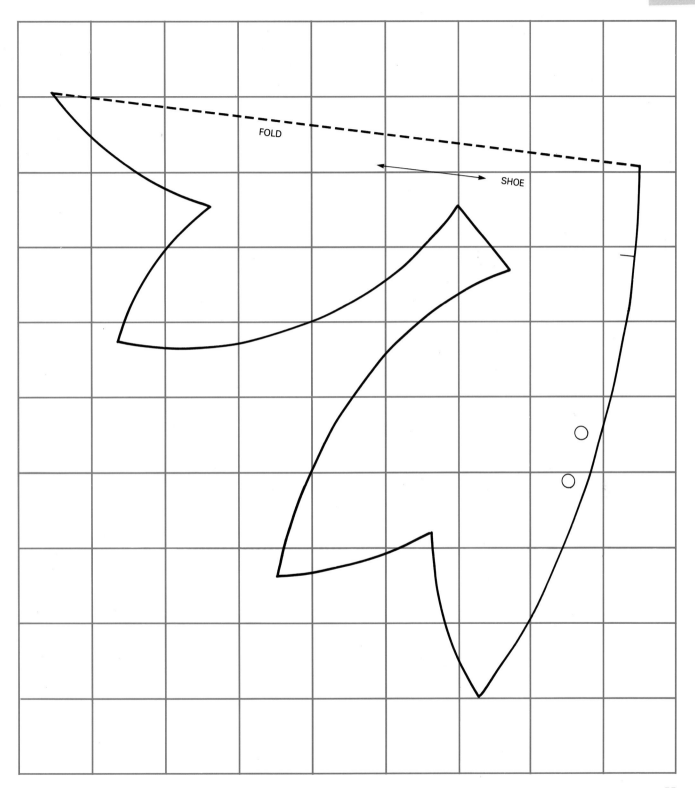

FOLD

SHOE

15
Quilt-block budgie **

This quick and simple toy is folded from a single pieced and quilted square block. Small, it can be a tiny doll or purse; a large version can serve as a pillow cover.

Piecing

Cut eight identical triangles, four each of two prints or colours. Cut one square of contrast fabric.

Join triangles to form quilt block. First, separate the triangles into four pairs of contrasting fabrics. Place each pair with right sides together. Stitch along the longest sides to form squares. Join the squares into two rectangles, and then join the two rectangles to form a single pieced square with the colours arranged as shown. When piecing the squares together, ensure that the seams match exactly. Press seams open.

Place the completed quilt block on the contrasting block, right sides together. Cut a triangular piece of wadding half the size of the pieced block. Place the wadding underneath the two fabric blocks. Tack in place. Stitch around the outside edges of the layered blocks and wadding, leaving an opening for turning.

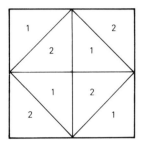 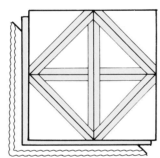

Trim wadding close to the seams. Clip corners. Turn right side out. Ease out corners gently from inside. Sew opening closed.

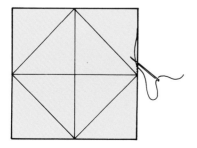

You now have a pieced half-padded block that will be folded into the bird shape. To make the folding process easier and to give some additional stability, quilt the block by stitching close to the outside edges and along the seams of the pieced block (stitch-in-the-ditch). You will notice that one triangular half of the block is padded and that the other half is not. The padded part will eventually form the head and upper wings of the bird; the lower part will become the feet. Stitch along the additional lines indicated, positioning the padded part of the square so that it receives the parallel ridges and that the unpadded part receives the small interior rectangle.

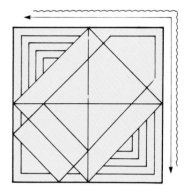

Place the quilted block flat on a table in front of you so that the corners are vertical, giving a diamond shape. Place the square so that the ridged parallel quilting lines are at your left and right and that the small quilted rectangle is nearest you. Fold carefully according to the diagrams. (You may want to try this with a square of paper first so that you understand the folds more clearly.)

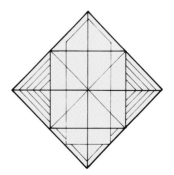

1 Bring point **C** to centre point **E**. Fold.
2 Bring point **A** to centre of line **HG**. Fold.
3 Fold this flap up again along line **HG**. (First fold will be inside.)

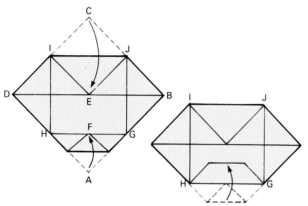

4 Bring points **D** and **B** to centre **E**. Fold.
5 (Note that the diamond shape has become a square.) Fold the sides of this square backwards so that they meet in the centre back. Let the edges of the triangles fall flat at the sides to form the wings.

6 Turn over. Bring lower points **G** and **H** to meet points **B** and **D**, folding along lines indicated and flattening the bottom edge into a boat shape.

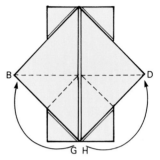

7 There are now little pockets formed at **G** and **H**. Fold these down along the lines indicated so that the edges lie along the centre axis. These flaps will form the feet.
8 Turn over. This completes the basic bird shape.

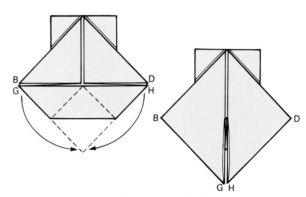

To fix the foot folds in place, pin and then sew the edges of the folded flaps together. Then sew together the folds from the centre along the centre back axis to the top.

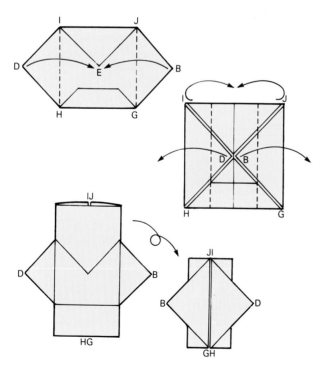

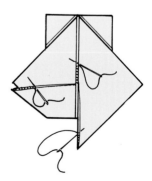

Turn bird over. Curve wings and bill up slightly by rolling gently around a pencil or knitting needle.

Fold feet up and sew in place if desired, or leave them flat and movable.

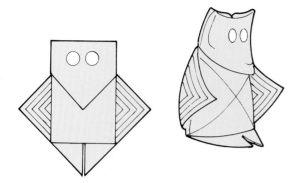

For eyes, cut circles of contrasting fabric. Work running stitch around the edges. Gather the edges around a small button to shape eye. Press. Remove button. Fill with a little wadding and pull the thread tight. Fasten off. Flatten a little into padded circles and sew in place.

If the head is left unsewn, the bird can serve as a little pocket or purse, or the front and back of the head can be sewn together to form a solid shape.

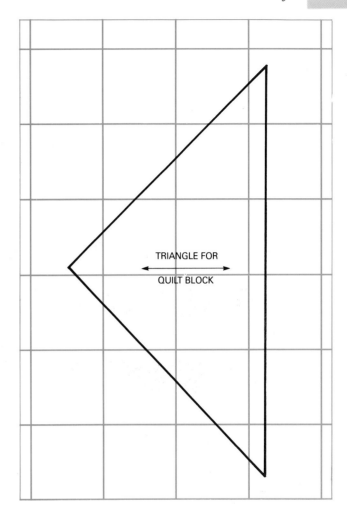

TRIANGLE FOR

QUILT BLOCK

Padded heart shapes of various sizes become the feet, body and head of this traditionally but simply strung bird marionette. Flexible bias tubes for legs and neck allow free and funny movements.

Feet and body

Mark shapes of all pieces on wrong sides of fabric or make templates to stitch around. Place fabric and facing, right sides together, on top of layer of wadding. Stitch through all layers, leaving opening for turning. Trim. Clip corners and curves and to stitching between two main curves at top of heart shape. Turn all pieces right sides out. Ease out edges from inside. Use knitting needle to ease out point. Roll edges gently between thumb and forefinger to define shape. (Do not press.) Handsew opening.

Quilt two largest body hearts and feet hearts by stitching close to edge. Stitch again at regular intervals following contour of heart.

Complete feet by stacking one heart on top of a second, matching edges exactly. Sew together at edges. Stitch to reinforce by stitching through both layers over outer rows of quilting.

Head

Prepare head heart as above, but do not quilt. Fold in half lengthwise. Sew edges together, leaving a gap at widest point for insertion of neck.

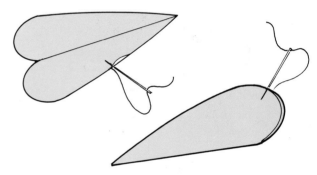

To form bill, fold a piece of yellow fabric right sides together. Using head pattern as a template, place fold line of pattern along fold of fabric. Stitch along lower edge for half the length of heart shape. Trim excess fabric. Clip point. Turn in raw edge. Press. Turn right side out. Slip over pointed end of folded heart. Sew in place.

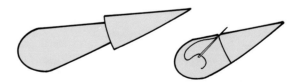

Assembling body

Pin smaller of two quilted hearts to top of larger, matching inner points. Sew hearts together from inner point, leaving lower pointed end free. Fold unsewn tip of larger heart against itself, and sew folded point together. Repeat with smaller heart. Pin small unquilted heart to other side of large heart, matching inner points. Join by sewing around edges. Fold layered hearts lengthwise to form body. Handsew curved front edges of largest heart together to form rounded front of body.

Neck and legs

Fold bias strips for neck and legs lengthwise, right sides together. Stitch long edges together, leaving one end open for turning. Trim. Turn right sides out. Turn in raw edges on ends and hand sew.

Sew legs to centre top of feet and to inside of body. Insert neck inside head. Sew sides of neck to head and to centre front of body (inner point of folded heart).

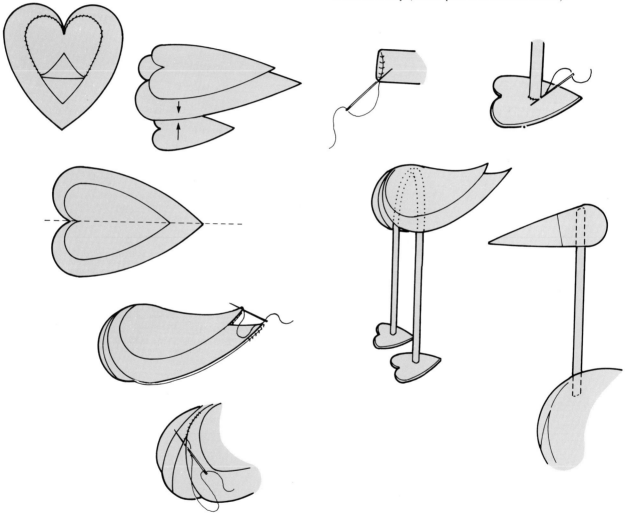

Feathers

Mark feather shapes on right side of fabric or make a template to stitch around. Place layer of wadding between fabric and facing (right sides out). Stitch through all layers. Zigzag over first stitching. Trim close to stitching. Satin stitch around edges, stretching slightly as you stitch to form ruffled edge. Sew feathers to head.

Before gluing pieces together, wrap ends of long strings around the ends of each long half dowel. Glue strings in place. Allow to dry. Glue top sections to long bar. Allow to dry. Attach strings of long rod to body and head as shown, adjusting length of strings as necessary. Attach strings to crossbar in the same way. Attach crossbar strings to middle of leg strips, forming 'knees'. (The leg strings should be roughly two times longer than the head string. The head string should be about three-quarters the length of the body string.)

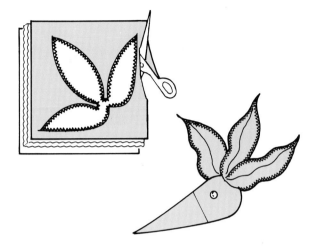

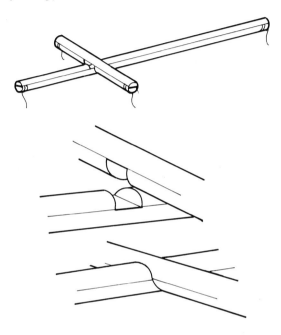

Rods and strings

Form marionette rods from pieces of narrow half-dowel glued together. Each piece consists of one uncut piece and second and third pieces positioned so that one end is flush with one end of the uncut rod, leaving a space the width of the dowel between them. This space will allow the rod and crossbar to fit together.

To work marionette

Hold long rod in one hand. Manipulate head by lowering or raising the head end of the long rod. Manipulate the feet by working the crossbar separately in up and down and back and forth movements. This takes a little practice, but soon you will be able to make the heartbird walk about quite comfortably.

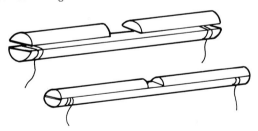

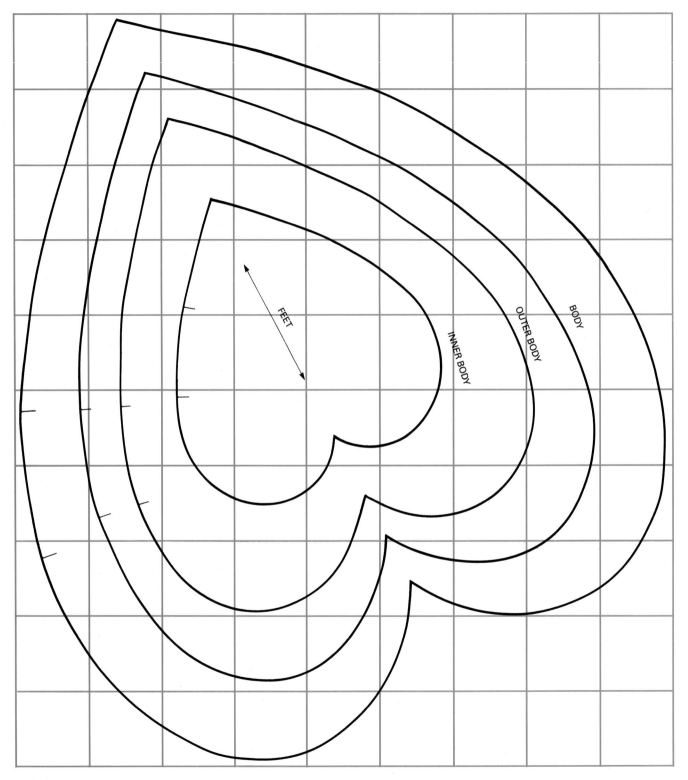

FEET

INNER BODY

OUTER BODY

BODY

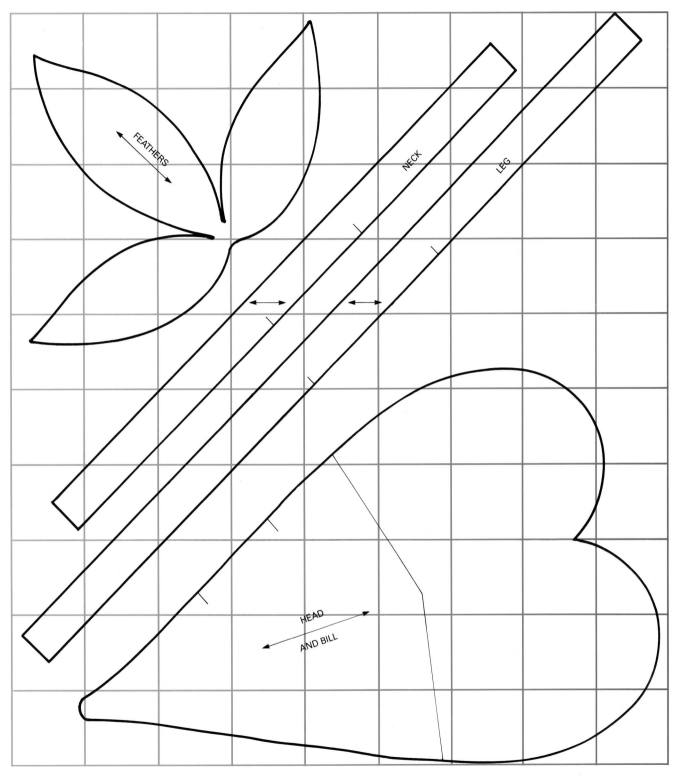

FEATHERS

NECK

LEG

HEAD
AND BILL

17
Car ***

The car consists of two parts: a wagon with a detachable handle and coiled quilted wheels that turn, and an upper body shell which fits over the base to form the sides and roof.

Wagon base

The wagon has three parts: a cross-shaped quilted base whose arms fold up to form the sides of the wagon; a quilted base lining which reinforces the wagon base; and wheels, axles and axle cases attached to the bottom of the wagon base.

Mark wagon, liner, axles and axle case shapes on wrong side of fabric or cut templates to stitch around. Place right sides of fabric and facing together. Place on top of wadding. Stitch through all layers, leaving opening for turning. Trim all pieces close to stitching. Clip corners. Turn inside out. Ease corners out from inside. Ease seam edges out by rolling gently between thumb and forefinger (do not press). Topstitch edges of liner and wagon. Quilt liner and wagon at regular intervals as desired, pinning and tacking to keep layers from puckering.

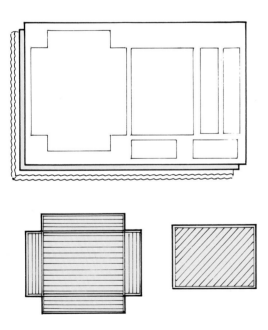

Axle

Zigzag all over surface of turned axle shape to stiffen. Fold in half lengthwise. Zigzag again through all layers to form a stiff narrow strip. Fold again lengthwise. Zigzag over edge (or hand sew if too bulky for machine) to form axle rod. Ease into round shape by rolling between fingers.

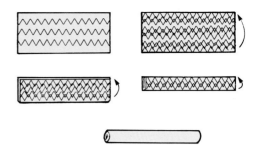

Axle case

Zigzag over entire surface of turned axle case rectangle to stiffen. Stitch piece of clear vinyl or any slippery fabric to one side of axle case. Stitch at crosswise intervals to fasten. Place one edge, slippery surface uppermost, along axle line indicated on wagon base. Stitch to base.

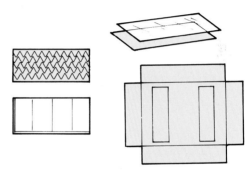

Bring opposite edge to stitched edge. Using narrow zigzag, stitch new edge to wagon base. (Slippery surface is now enclosed inside axle case.) Bring centre fold to position above stitched edges. Fold sides down against base so that cylindrical 'tunnel' is formed inside axle case. Tack. Test size of opening by inserting axle through casing. Check to see that it moves freely. Remove axle. Stitch in place through all layers. If correctly stitched, case will form cylindrical opening to hold axle, with slippery surface inside.

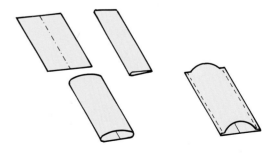

Place liner over inside wagon surface. Sew to base along edges. Fold sides of wagon base up to form sides of wagon. Sew together by hand, securing corners firmly. If desired, bind entire top edge with bias binding to reinforce.

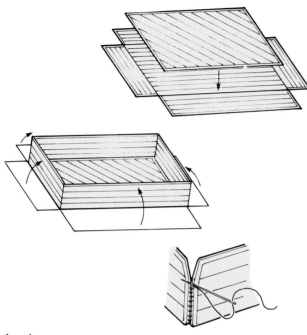

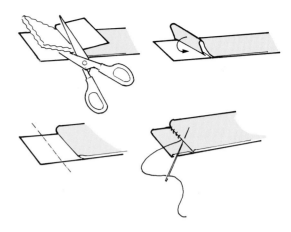

Wheels

Mark strips along bias (cross) on wrong side of fabric. (Note that strips must be at least twice the length of pattern piece; size of wheels can be varied by changing this length.) Place right sides of fabric and facing together. Place on top of wadding. Stitch through all layers, leaving one end open for turning. Trim. Clip corners. Turn inside out. Trim open end of padded strip so that one surface is slightly longer than the other. Remove a little wadding under longer edge to make thin layer for finishing. Turn longer surface under (this will form the final surface of the wheel, and needs to be thinner in order to make the wheel round when wound up.) Handsew to close. Stitch along strip lengthwise through all layers to secure.

To form wheel, stitch unaltered end of strip to end of axle. (Check exact position of wheels on axle by placing axle through axle case. Adjust so that ends of axle project equally. Position end of wheel strip at least 2 mm ($^1/_{16}$ inch) away from side of wagon so that when sewn in position, wheel can move freely. Wheel should just meet end of axle, but can overlap it slightly.)

Roll wheel strip tightly around axle rod, so that rolled layers grow into wheel shape. As you roll the strip, take a few hand stitches at regular intervals to secure strip in place. Be careful to roll exactly so that separate edges do not project. Pin tapered end of strip to last layer and handsew invisibly to secure. Place axle through axle case. Attach opposite wheel in same way, being careful to wind the wheel strip with the same degree of tension so that wheels end up the same size.

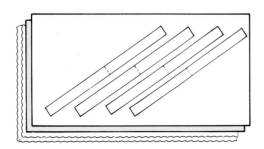

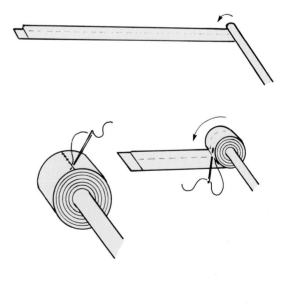

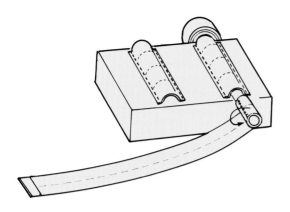

Stitch seam. Press seam allowance open. Turn under raw edges to make narrow hem. Then fold both hems in to meet in centre, making sure that width of tread band exactly matches width of wheel. Slipstitch edges together. Slip band over wheel.

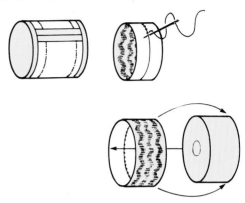

Treads

Because the size of the coiled wheel will vary according to the tension of winding, there is no pattern piece for the tread. To determine size of tread piece, measure circumference of finished wheel with piece of thread as shown. Add enough for seam allowance (about 10 mm (½ inch)). Cut piece of bias fabric (on the cross) to this length and twice as wide as wheel plus a narrow seam allowance. Attach three parallel rows of tiny rickrack to centre of strip to form tread. Fold in half crosswise, matching edges of rickrack carefully. Mark. Check measurement by wrapping strip around wheel. Marks should just meet for snug fit. Adjust if necessary.

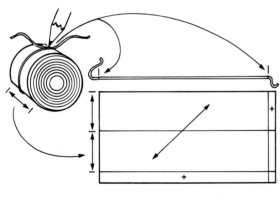

Handle

Fold handle strip lengthwise, right sides together. Place on layer of wadding. Stitch. Trim. Turn right sides out. Stitch along length of handle. Fold in half lengthwise. Zigzag edges together. Fold in half crosswise. Stitch lengthwise in centre of strip, leaving loop open at folded end for handle. Fold loop flat into handle shape and hand sew to secure. Use large hook and eye to fasten handle to wagon. (Sew handle on if for use by very young children. An alternative method is to work a second T-shape handle at lower end, and a buttonhole in one of the short wagon sides. The handle will then be retractable when car top is used.)

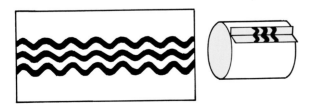

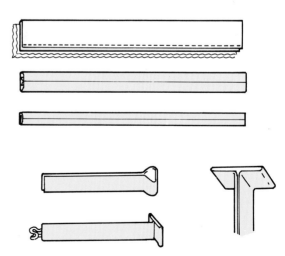

Car top

Topstitch along lower edge and other marked lines. Mark shapes of sides and top of car on wrong side of fabric, or make templates to stitch around. Place right sides of fabric and facing together; .place on top of wadding. Stitch through all layers, leaving opening for turning. Trim; clip corners and curves. Turn inside out. Ease corners from inside. (Do not press.) Handsew opening. Work narrow zigzag along window lines of side and top pieces. Stitch along quilting lines of sides and top of car. Cut out window centres, trimming close to stitching. Satin-stitch along window edges, being careful not to stretch edges. Place pieces of transparent vinyl beneath side and top windows. Stitch along window edges, along outer edge of satin stitch, away from opening, fastening vinyl in for window. Trim vinyl close to stitching. Join sides to centre by hand, matching edges, or join by zigzagging with right sides together.

Make headlights by working small running stitch around edge of headlight circles. Place penny in centre. Gather around penny by pulling thread. Press. Remove penny. Pad slightly by putting a small amount of stuffing inside. Sew edges together to secure. Pin in place on front of car. Sew invisibly to car top.

Remove wagon handle. Slip car top over wagon base to complete car.

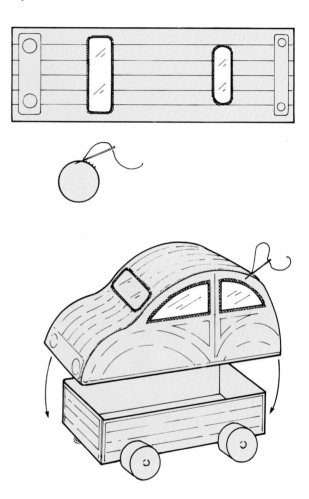

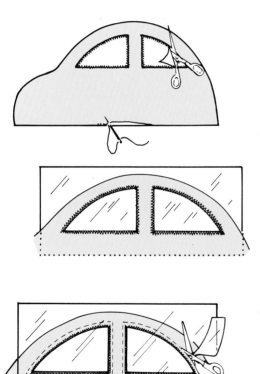

WAGON
BASE

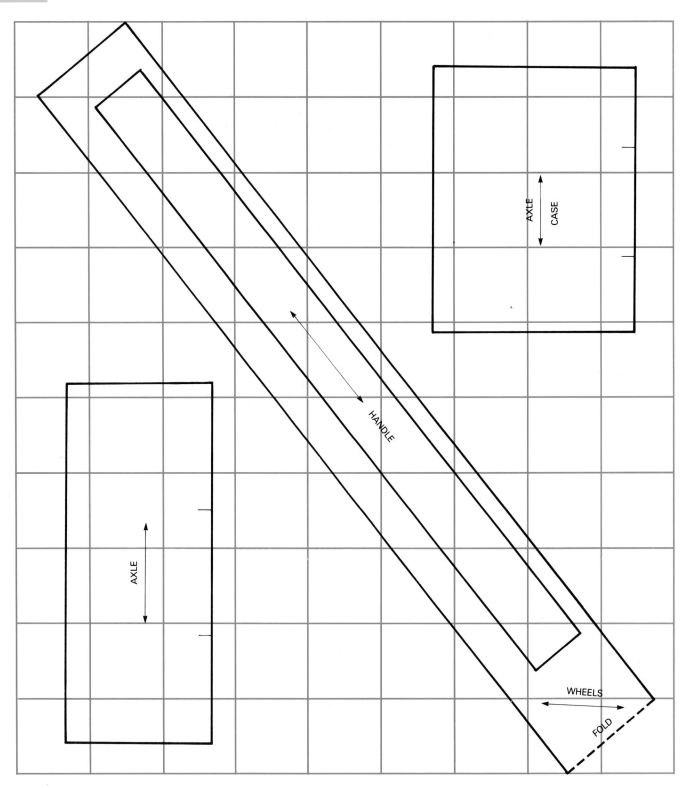

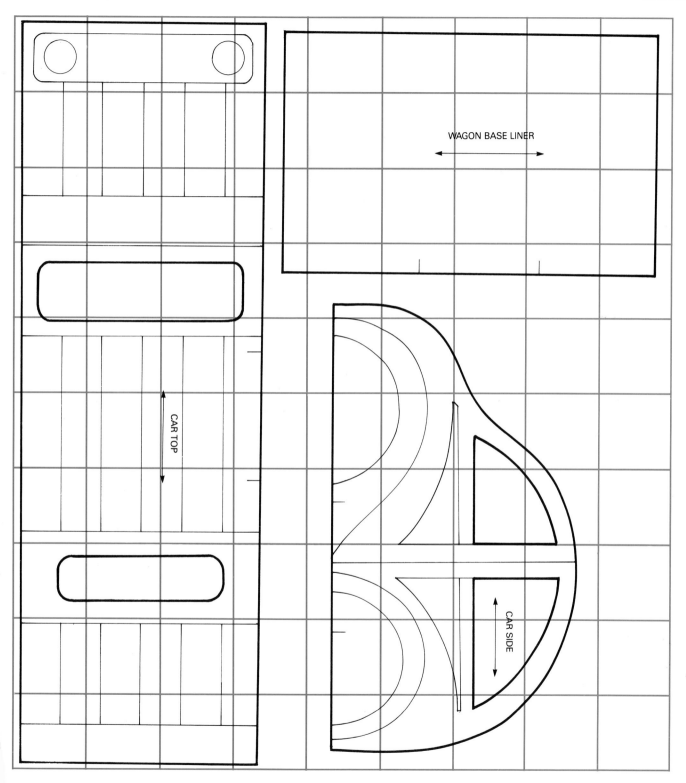

WAGON BASE LINER

CAR TOP

CAR SIDE

Further reading

While there are many books of soft toy patterns available, some including patchwork techniques, we have not encountered any that use quilting as a primary means of providing structure and stability as well as decoration.

Likewise, the wealth of books on quilting techniques rarely cover their application to toys.

However, we would like to suggest several authors whose books present particularly well designed or original toy pattern ideas. The experienced soft-toy-maker will probably already be familiar with the designs of Jean Greenhowe and Pamela Peake. An especially well designed series of toy patterns appears in the small Ondori books from Japan.

Other sources that could be useful to the reader who wishes to experiment with fabric construction and pattern design are the books of Carolyn Hall and Toni Scott. Perhaps the best sources for inventive ideas in the sculptural use of textiles are the series of *Fiberarts Design Books* and the periodicals *Threads* and *Fiberarts*. Many women's magazines also run craft features; of the ones that are consistently interesting, we like the American publication *Women's Day*.

Adult Education Institutes often run related courses in textiles and soft sculpture structures. One we would particularly like to recommend is Victoria Bartlett's class at Morley College in London. Her sculptural work in fabric and paper has been a constant source of inspiration, and her classes at Morley have become a kind of forum for innovative exploration in the use of textiles and other soft materials.